Requests for permission to make copies of any
part of the work should be submitted online
to info@mascotbooks.com or mailed to:

Mascot Books
560 Herndon Parkway #120
Herndon, VA 20170.

ISBN: 1-936319-08-X
CPSIA Code: PRT0910A

Printed in the United States

www.mascotbooks.com

Parent & Student Guide to College Admissions

All You Need to Know to Prepare Your Child for the College Application Process

By Esther H. Scheuer, MS

Dedication

My deepest thanks goes to my loving husband of forty-three years, Herb, who supported me unconditionally, even with computer glitches, while writing this book. I am grateful to all of the parents who gave me the opportunity to work with their children and to their sons and daughters, who I learned so much from. I will be forever grateful for my four wonderful daughters, Laura, Beth, Amy, and Jennifer, who not only taught me what I needed to know in order to help other children, but have allowed me to be a part of their lives as adults. Their love and support help me to accomplish my goals with others. It would be remiss to leave out my son-in-law, Bryan Rader, who was kind and generous with his time taken to edit this book. In addition, to my good friend, John Hartsfield, who also took the time to read and edit as well, I give my sincere thanks. And last, but not least, I dedicate this book to my 10 grandchildren, Jessica, Austin, Carter, Davis, Reese, Ben, Sara, Rachel, Morgan and Molly, whom I love dearly.

Notes From the Author

My motivation in developing this book was driven by my concern for families of college bound students. Over the last fifteen years as a high school counselor and independent counselor, I have observed the high anxiety of parents and students dealing with the college selection and application process. Their struggle with choosing the right school that is a good match academically, socially and financially can be overwhelming—especially for parents going through the process for the first time.

In my lengthy career as a counselor, I had come across many parents frustrated by the time it would take to research college possibilities, give advice on essays, timelines, scholarships, financial aid and the process in general. Students were apprehensive about being accepted and dreaded organizing all the paper work it was going to take; applications, essays, recommendations, developing a resume, visiting colleges and auditioning for scholarships. All of this concerned the parents with how their senior would be able to incorporate all of these details in an orderly and timely manner, especially with school work demands and extracurricular activities. The high anxiety of the unknown in this process affects the entire family.

In compiling all of the information on the college application process, coupled with my own experiences, this book gives a step-by-step guide for students and parents during the application process.

I empathize with each of you who are entering this process, and my hope in writing this book is to provide guidance and advice that will alleviate some of your fears about your college selection—while making the overall process easier for you and leading you toward a more successful outcome.

Table of Contents

INTRODUCTION

Throughout my life and my career as a professional counselor, I've seen the college admission process change dramatically. In the 1960s, the idea of going to college seemed simple. If you were on the college academic track, you would make decent grades, take a standardized test (didn't prepare or worry about the score), fill out the application and you were accepted! Oh, and by the way, it was usually to your state university, so the cost was less and the decision easy. Using a counselor (most of us didn't even know there was such a position) to help or suggest other options was rare. In fact, there was a door that was always closed in my high school—rumor had that it that a counselor occupied the space. But, nobody ever saw her. Today, counselors are not only visible and more knowledgeable about colleges, scholarships, and standardized testing, students must know where the counselor's office is in their high school and tend to utilize the counselors services much more today than in the past. As with any profession, there are good and bad counselors; those who care and those who do not, as well as those who have more knowledge than others.

When I became a parent, I knew that one day my children would go to college. Quicker than I could blink an eye, the time arrived for our first daughter to apply. She not only talked about her interest in a career of fashion merchandising, which meant researching more extensive programs, but she also wanted to go out-of-state, two issues I'd never thought would be considered. How would we pay for an out-of-state school? Who could I ask for advice? I had lots of questions and wasn't sure where to find answers.

Computers had been in existence for a short while, so using the web helped. Books did too, but these means only provided us with application requirements, deadlines, majors, campus organizations, college costs, and other facts about each college we researched. I needed to know a lot more. Who could analyze her scores, grades, interests, abilities, and her strengths and weaknesses, academically and socially?

My daughter attended a very large public high school—her counselor was responsible for hundreds of students, and was up to her elbows in paper work. She wasn't very knowledgeable about the out-of-state schools and didn't know much about my daughter. I knew it was up to me to do it all. After surveying colleges online, writing for brochures and applications, comparing details of programs and costs, speaking with other students who had or were presently attending her schools of interests and visiting schools in various areas of the country, she decided to attend Stephens College in Columbia, Missouri.

When my second daughter was sixteen years old, she began to talk about colleges and universities she'd heard about at summer camp. Of course, they were also out-of-state colleges and once again the same concerns were in play. This time, I thought I would be better prepared. Wrong! It was just as difficult. Her academic profile, goals and aspirations were totally different from those of my oldest daughter—as were her needs. She attended the same public high school as her older sister, so I knew there wouldn't be much help from the counselor. Between researching on the web, reading college books and traveling to schools, we started the application process. She attended the University of Colorado in Boulder, Colorado.

We switched our last two children to a private school. My third daughter, five years behind my second daughter, began private school in the ninth grade and before we knew it, she too was college bound. This time, I really thought there'd be a counselor I could look to for help with the application process. Wrong again! This counselor wasn't very helpful in the process either. Once again, I began the research process. She was an experienced ballerina who danced for the local professional ballet company and was trained in two summer programs. One was at the Joffrey in New York City and the other at the Boston Ballet. So now, we had to look for two additional criteria: Academics (she was a strong academic student) and dance. We traveled to many schools in the East, Midwest and the South. As we continued our search, she decided that she wanted to place more emphasis on academics, but still continue dancing. She chose the University of Georgia in Athens, Georgia. She was awarded the top dance scholarship as well as being admitted into the honors program.

My last daughter, who attended the same private school as my third daughter, was also interested in out-of-state colleges. Her strength was writing and her interests and talents varied from sports to voice. She researched and visited various schools in the Midwest because they were known for good journalism schools. She attended the University of Kansas in Lawrence, Kansas.

In the eleven years between the first daughter and the last daughter, the competition for college admissions grew. This prompted me to help each child prepare more rigorously in terms of standardized testing and curriculum development.

In addition, as time progressed and each experience I had with another college search, I began to become aware of factors beyond just the application process. As each of my daughters went through the process of researching colleges, I found that I was not prepared emotionally. I couldn't stop thinking about the tools needed to deal with all the things that came with college. The questions that kept me up at night were:

- Will she get enough *sleep*?

- What if she gets *sick*?

- Will someone slip a ***drug in her drink?***

- Will she be able to keep up with her ***dirty clothes***?

- Will she be responsible with *no curfews* or limits?

- Will she be safe from a random *rapist* on campus?

- Will she use the *campus police* escort if she is out late at the library?

- Will she engage in *casual sex*?

- Will she drink too much *alcohol*?

- Will she use *drugs*?

- Will she manage the *level of college work* required?

- Will she *join a sorority*?

- Will she live in a *dorm* or in an *apartment*?

- Will she meet a *special boy*?

- Will she be able to keep up with her *academics*?

These questions are normal—parents can't help but worry about the unlearned life skills their children will have to learn in college. But, life skills are an ongoing learning process. Even though they can't all be taught before a child leaves for college, some can be addressed during the college application process.

Students' Immediate Concerns

High School students have many concerns while researching and applying to colleges. This process and the results are so exposing that the pressure alone can make *a teenager fly off the handle.* So, one can expect a level of *friction* between the parent and the high school student. He/she is trying to collect information about colleges, fill out those applications, keep up higher grades, and manage the "social pressures" that come during that process.

In Addition, Friends Will Ask:

- "What college are you going to *next year*?"

- "How many colleges are you *applying* to?"

- "Did you apply for any *scholarships*? You know I know of one..."

- "If you don't *keep up your grades your entire senior year*, it can affect the decision a college may have made in the fall."

- "Are you going to go *'early action'* or *'early decision'*?"

- "Have you taken a *college tour* yet?"

- "Have you looked at the *deadlines*?"

- "Do you want to go *out-of-state for college*?"

- "Do you want to go to a school where your *friends will attend*?"

During this time, students contend with these outside pressures from others along with ongoing school demands as well as extracurricular responsibilities (possibly a job). It is hard, but especially necessary for them to think about themselves in order to be effective in the college application process. So self-awareness is something every student needs help with.

Self-Awareness and Self-Evaluation for the Student

The following questions will help you focus on yourself as an individual, as well as on your future choices. An honest and thoughtful self-evaluation can reveal what you should look for in a college. This will prepare you for statements you may be asked to make about yourself in essays and interviews when you apply. A serious look at yourself will help you find the options that are right for you as well as help you present yourself effectively to college admission professionals. The following questions are ones that you, the student, need to address:

Goals

1. What aspects of your high school years have been most meaningful to you?

2. If you could live this period over again, would you do anything differently?

3. What do you care most about?

4. What occupies most of your energy, effort, and/or thoughts?

5. How do you define success?

6 Are you satisfied with your accomplishments to date?

7. What do you want to accomplish in the years ahead?

8. What kind of person would you like to become?

9. Of your unique gifts and strengths, which would you like to develop?

10. What would you most like to change about yourself?

11. Is there anything you have ever secretly wanted to do or be?

12. If you had a year to go anywhere and do whatever you wanted, how would you spend it?

13. What experiences have shaped your growth and way of thinking?

Education

1. What are your academic interests?

2. Which courses have you enjoyed the most?

3. Which courses have been most difficult for you and why?

4. What do you choose to learn when you can learn on your own? Consider interests pursued beyond class assignments: topics chosen for research papers, lab reports, independent projects; independent reading; school activities; job or volunteer work.

5. What do your choices show about your interests and the way you like to learn?

6. How do you learn best?

7. What methods of teaching and style of teacher engages your interest the most?

8. How much do you genuinely like to read, discuss issues, and exchange ideas?

9. What has been your most stimulating intellectual experience in recent years?

10. How would you describe your school?

11. Is learning and academic success in your school respected?

12. Has the school's environment encouraged you to develop your interests, talents, and abilities?

13. Have you felt limited in any way?

14. What would you preserve or change about the school if you were able to do so?

15. How well has your school prepared you for college?

16. In what areas of skills or knowledge do you feel most confident or least confident?

17. Have you been challenged by your courses?

18. Have you worked up to your potential?

19. Is your academic record an accurate measure of your ability and potential?

20. Are you satisfied with your ACT or SAT scores?

21. What do you consider the best measures of your potential for college work?

22. Are there any outside circumstances (in your recent experience or background) which have interfered with your academic performance? Consider such factors as: after-school jobs, home responsibilities or difficulties, excessive school activities, illness or emotional stress, parental influences, or other factors which are unique to your background.

How to Choose a College

Choosing the right college can seem like the most important decision you'll ever make. After all, your college education will affect the rest of your life. It can be scary. I know your fears. "What if I make the wrong choice? What if I'm not happy there? What if I don't learn anything? What if I don't get in?"

Relax! There is no one magic choice. There are likely to be many institutions at which you would be happy. And if you're not, you can always transfer to another college for your sophomore or junior year. Your first year, experiences will aid you in making a more informed choice for your next school. The most common reason for unhappiness during the first year at college is difficulty getting along with one's roommate. If this is the case, try to find solutions through resident assistants, counselors, and other helpers in your dorm or at the college. If you're still unhappy, try changing roommates. Often, however, freshman roommates remain friends for life.

The only poor college choices are the ones made without enough information. An excellent source of information is your high school college admissions office or an independent counselor (a hired private counselor that provides guidance throughout the college planning and application process).

The college admission counselor or independent counselor will have available a variety of handbooks with descriptions of colleges. If you're not sure what you want to do, your counselor can help you clarify what your interests and talents are. Afterwards, you can search the college websites online or use college handbooks to gather information about each specific college.

At Some Point, You Will Be Answering Six Questions:

1. ***What kind of college do I want to attend?*** A liberal arts school or a pre-professional school?

2. ***What size school do I want?*** For example, a school with 10,000 students or more or one with as few as several hundred.

3. ***Where do I want to be?*** Staying close to home or going far away? Some people find being far away too lonely; others enjoy the freedom. Sometimes staying close eliminates the problem of adjusting to a new environment; sometimes being too close keeps you in old ruts.

4. ***What location do I want?*** You can choose between urban or rural (big town or small town). Urban schools create an environment where there is noise and movement. Rural colleges offer lovely, quiet campuses. For some people, these are the best places to study; for others they're not.

5. ***What lifestyle do I want?*** There are conservative schools, liberal schools, fraternity/sorority oriented schools, gung-ho football schools, and religiously oriented schools. They all give you an education. Consider the kind of education you want, as well as what you want surrounding you when you're not studying.

6. ***What special programs or services do I want?*** Try to identify colleges offering activities and resources in which you are interested or have a need.

Questions and Answers

One of the questions asked most frequently is, "What should my final list of colleges include?" Inherent in this question are two considerations: first, how many schools should I apply to, and second, what range of schools should be included with regard to admissions competition?

Students should not adopt the "shotgun approach" of applying to a multitude of schools. Neither should students, regardless of academic ability, "put all of their eggs in one basket" by applying to only one institution or one academic level. As a general rule, students should apply to approximately three to six schools which vary in terms of selectivity, but which have the most important features desired by the student. Generally, it is recommended that a student's final list include schools from each of the following categories:

- **REACH** — A student's top choice schools. It is fine in this group to include a couple of long shots.

- **REALISTIC** — Schools that possess the significant features a student desires and the probability of admission is even slightly better than even. These are categorized as "realistic" schools.

- **SURE-BET** — These are schools that a student will definitely qualify for admissions, which includes their GPA and scores.

CHAPTER 1

Tracking in the Eighth Grade

So many decisions need to be made before even contemplating the college application process. It's best to start from the beginning.

While the development of a GPA for college applications begins in the ninth grade, students make choices in middle school that put them on higher level math and science tracks. By selecting a higher core curriculum, you will need to be aware of the way in which colleges view your choices. If you choose the most rigorous curriculum and do not make as high a grade, the college will value your academic challenge. You must, however, decide if this academic challenge fits your ability to make a decent grade (B or above). So, your GPA is effective in admission decisions relative to your course curriculum, especially in highly competitive schools.

The following are some thoughts about how to approach course selection that will fit the need of *your academic ability, interest and willingness,* and a timeline that will add perspective in preparing for college applications. Your choices of tracking (regular or rigorous) will impact your high school experience and college choices.

8th Grade — Steps to Preparing for High School

Course Selection

In the eighth grade, you have the option to select courses leading to a higher math or science level. This is called **tracking.** This is only a placement, not classes that will figure in the student's GPA for college admissions. According to the level of academic achievement, teachers can recommend students to choose a more excelled academic track in the spring of the eighth grade. Think and talk about a four year academic plan for high school based on this tracking. To cover all bases for applying to competitive colleges, a student should consider all available honors track courses if they can handle the challenge.

Good Study Habits

The key to developing good study habits is the **will to do it.** Most students can learn a routine, but must have a reason to follow through. How to get a student to believe in themselves is a real challenge.

The ten step reality is:

1. The goal is to succeed.

2. The only way to reach this goal of success is to work hard.

3. Hard work is effective if methods are correct.

4. Methods are correct if they are taught and the student learns and practices.

5. Learning and practice are determined by willingness.

6. Willingness is present if there is purpose.

7. Purpose exists if there is a reason.

8. Reason is a fact if there is something to gain.

9. Gain is the key to willingness.

10. Willingness yields success.

Being An Active Parent

Parent Involvement

Guide your student to become involved in something in which he/she can become proficient. Give support by offering lessons, such as private sessions. Plus, find a friend or peer for mentoring. Let's say your student wants to compete for cheerleading. Find a girl who is already a cheerleader and have her teach her the ropes and how to try out successfully. Parents are not always the best choice for teaching their children. *Your efforts in making sure they have the resources needed are an important part of the equation.*

Group Involvement

Encourage friendships that will lead to group involvement. One way to do this is to find out about organizations like Tri-Hi-Y. As a parent, conduct research so you're informed enough to help guide your student into joining. Speak with mothers of other students who you know will join and make it seem like "the thing to do." Then offer to be part of the carpool and find out about the events planned. You can also speak with older student members to understand what your student can do to participate in the future or rise to leadership positions. *This information is not meant for your involvement, but for your support and encouragement.*

Academics

Academics are areas where most students will need some assistance at one time or another. *Providing tutors, (adult or student), will increase the student's confidence in an area that may be weak.*

Activity List—Make a List of High School Activities

Parents should familiarize themselves with the many possible activities, clubs and organizations available to their high school student. Go to the high school counselor's office and ask for these lists. Some are obvious, but others like the National Honor Society have requirements for membership and benefits like scholarships for college. Your high school student may be offered similar lists, but your knowledge will help in discussing and teaching your student how to plan for high school in this area and why. If you don't have time to go to the counselor's office, you might find some of this information at your high schools web-site. Resumés begin to count in the ninth grade, and therefore you should begin thinking toward the end of the eighth grade about where the high school student needs to be placed to get the best educational experience (not everything is learned in a book).

> **Tidbit:** *Without self-confidence, a student will find school to be painful and unfulfilling. One only feels successful when something has been accomplished. Accomplishment is the path to success. And this is incredibly important, starting in the eighth grade.*

CHAPTER 2

9ᵗʰ Grade: Setting Up for High School

Select the 9ᵗʰ Grade Curriculum

As a parent you need to know that each grade has a special impact on a student's future.

High school students generally become concerned about the college process in their junior year as the time approaches for the **spring standardized testing**. By the time they realize they want to apply to a highly competitive school, they are already in the process of taking junior year courses. It is important for you, the parents, to discuss course curriculum choices prior to each grade, starting in the eighth grade, as mentioned before. If you, the student, have chosen to take a regular core curriculum track, then you decided from the beginning of your course selection in the eighth grade to continue this track through high school. This is fine if you know that you are academically comfortable with a regular core curriculum. You can add more academic electives such as Psychology or add AP (Advanced Placement) courses. You will not, however, be in a position with other students who chose to take a more rigorous track that will allow them the opportunity for more competitive colleges. So, when choosing your academic electives, be sure and research any colleges that you may want to apply to for admissions about their level of competitiveness in the application process. Therefore, it is important to be informed and positive in planning the type of academic schedule that *you* will follow early on.

Tracking determines if you will be able to take more advanced classes. So the eighth grade course selection will affect *your* ninth grade track and course selection. Honors and any AP courses that are offered should be selected if you are going to consider competitive schools. It is best to keep *your* options open. Depending on the number of AP courses that are offered and taken by typical students, *you* should be competitive in *your* selection. *The strength of your course load will be noted by your high school counselor on the Counselor Evaluation Form of your applications to college.*

Factors for 9th Graders to Consider

Study Skills

The Development of Good Study Skills: Have a notebook per subject with pockets for syllabus and extra sheets pertaining to any special project or paper required in any given course.

Study Schedule

The development of a study schedule that will:

- Help you review notes for discussion classes each night.

- Organize time for homework.

- Use 3" x 5" index cards to record classroom notes and save them for final exam studying.

- Buy a calendar to record any large projects due and a schedule to work on the project.

- Become involved with extra curricular activities that may lead to leadership positions in upper grades (more about this later).

- Begin developing a resume that can be supplemental. Save on a thumb drive or CD.

- Create time for you to have a social time during the afternoon or evening.

- Keep involvement reasonable in accordance with your academic load.

Summer Job

Take a Summer Job: Choosing a job in an area of interest to you gives you the experience to find out if that particular field is appealing in terms of a possible career. Some jobs put you in positions of leadership like being a camp counselor, life guard or babysitter. Other jobs are volunteer based – ones that are charitable (non-profits) and don't earn money but do provide a valuable experience. ***Also, competitive colleges like to see that you have a sense of responsibility***.

Resumé

Start Working on a Resumé: Using ***word processing*** on a computer allows for additions of any new information such as activities, awards, etc. Talk with a counselor to find a format that will be acceptable by colleges. ***Resumé format found in Chapter II.***

Travel

When you travel, drop-in and ***visit college campuses*** in the area. You can visit the homepage of any college or university to schedule a tour and information session. However, this step is optional at this time.

College Savings Account

Parents need to start a plan for college funding. Today, there are many options available for all cost levels.

Scholarships

Investigate possible scholarships so **you** are ready to start applying in the tenth grade. The counselors office in the high school is a good place to start, as well as private scholarships found online or associated with organizations or religious affiliations.

Extracurricular Activities

Quantity is not important. What is important to colleges and to your self development is a **three-to-four year commitment**. Having a variety of clubs, sports, teams, etc. is fine to participate in and is part of being well rounded. **But, for selective colleges, long-term commitments are favored over a long resumé and a well- rounded student is not as important as a well- rounded freshman class. "Quality is generally preferred over quantity."**

Class Participation

You should show interest in the classroom by **volunteering comments or asking related questions**. If you are shy, prepare a question or two before class. Make sure you are **prepared for class** and have done your homework and assignments. It is important to show that you are **interested** in learning and not just doing your work for a high grade. Teachers will fill in boxes ("Effective participation in class") on Teacher Recommendation Forms for college. They will have to answer questions such as, "Will this student add to our college? What kind of impact will this student have?" How is the student's participation in your class? **Colleges, especially selective ones, want to know if you, the student, will contribute to the classroom or raise the level of discussion and are not there just to make a grade.**

Summertime

Read as much as you can to increase your vocabulary. Materials can range from newspapers, magazines, scientific journals, novels, fiction books, etc. This will prepare you for the **verbal content** on standardized tests like the **SAT I** and the **ACT.** Find a short- term course in a **top summer school**. Continue adding to your list of **activities throughout this stage of your college preparation**.

CHAPTER 3

10th Grade: Developing Personal Growth

During the sophomore year, students should begin to **recognize their strengths and weaknesses academically**. Just as important, they should be able to **identify their interests and abilities**. In addition, students should plan how to expand on these, always considering their aptitude. For example, I may play the flute, but at this point only play for my own amusement. If the student feels that this is an area that could be improved, then the student must plan to **set goals to achieve the level desired**. Not only will the student be able to utilize this talent when applying for colleges and scholarships, but will also project the image of devotion, commitment, sacrifice, and ability all in one package. This is **the year to develop personal growth.**

Academic Choices

College Search and Visit

If the high school schedules a college tour that sophomores can sign up for, do go. This will give you exposure to large and small colleges and universities, even if those schools chosen by the counselor are not of particular interest to you. If you decide to go Early Decision (binding) or Early Action (will receive acceptance or denial as early as December of your senior year) your familiarity with these campuses may help you with your choice.

Advanced Placement, Also Known as "AP"

If you have taken an AP course, you will want to take the AP test in the spring. The high school counselor will schedule this and inform you of the date(s).

Curriculum

Meet with the counselor to discuss the rigor of your chosen classes for your junior year and how that will impact on your possible college choices. Choosing honors courses will show that you challenged yourself. Making a "B" or above in an AP class is more acceptable then making an "A" in a less challenging course.

Foreign Language

In considering taking a third year of a foreign language, it is important to note that a third year may grant a student the opportunity to take a test during summer orientation at the school of choice, which will enable the student to either clep out (not required to take that course) or clep up (advance to the next level(s) of that course) in foreign language requirements.

College Fairs

Start visiting these fairs to gather information about the differences and similarities of schools. Also, make a list of the requirements (GPA, standardized scores, essay, curriculum, etc.) that each school requires. *This will help you focus while choosing a curriculum and making good grades.*

✓ Theme Development

A theme refers to any chosen activity that begins with your interest or talent. For example:

1. Begin with what you do at the present moment like *playing sports*.

2. Take *playing sports* and turn that into *teaching a little league team*.

3. Take *teaching a little league team* into developing a *program at a facility for underprivileged children to play sports in an after school day care*.

These "interest" themes that develop into leadership positions are what colleges respect and value the most on a resumé. This involvement can lead to information you address in your essay as well as recommendations.

Summer

Plan it with college in mind. Find a position or camp placement that allows you to implement your theme. Even if you pump gas, turn it into something creative like an idea of how to help improve customer service. *It is the quality of your time spent outside of class that the colleges are looking for in a resumé, not quantity.*

Standardized Testing

PLAN Test

The PLAN test *stimulates thinking and planning, assesses academic preparation and supports meaningful high school course selection for junior and senior years*. In addition, it relates personal characteristics to educational and career options. It can also help focus test preparation to *improve ACT scores* as well as provide an estimated ACT Assessment Composite score.

Parents

Pay attention to this first test in high school. It will *measure your high school student's ability to take standardized tests* and measure academic progress. You do this by going over the tests and noting what academic *areas need work*. For example, if in the math portion your student continually struggles on a certain step, ask the teacher to teach it again during a private session. This test contains an interest inventory, so use it to discuss with your student the value of its results. If there is an obvious area of interest, pursue it by arranging the opportunity for shadowing (being with a person in a specific career field to learn the everyday routine and what it entails). This way, a student becomes more knowledgeable about a desired career.

Students

There are only two words to say: "PAY ATTENTION." If you use this PLAN to *correct what you don't know* now, it will not only help you to do better in high school, but you will perform better on the ACT. So, when you get the test booklet and answer sheet back, evaluate what you missed and *take those questions to a teacher or another student* who scored well, and correct them. Not only do you learn about what you don't know, which will help you in school, but you will be better prepared the next time you take a standardized test.

There are a few goals of the PLAN that can be valuable early on, if students, parents and teachers treat it as such. According to ACT, students can:

- **Identify career and educational options**—Career evaluation is done through the ***Interest Inventory*** given as part of the PLAN. It contains a World-of-Work-Map with twenty-six career areas to help students find their strengths in the early stages of career exploration and planning. For educational options, this test can assess the ***status of educational achievement and weaknesses needed for the student to improve***. With this information, parents can help their student correct those academic weaknesses and therefore with the help of the counselor, decide upon course selection for the eleventh and twelfth grades.

- **Establish goals**—This raises the student awareness to identify career goals and pursue them through ***shadowing, personal development, or job opportunity***. This is very important when adding to the application process and one that will distinguish one student from another.

- **Determine courses to fulfill plans**—The test will help determine if a student should take another year of a science. This example guides the student in following the appropriated ***educational track*** at this time.

- **Evaluate educational/career progress**—This test monitors students' academic progress and can help them reach their post-high school goals.

Schedule for Taking the PLAN:

- Get plenty of ***sleep*** the night before.

- ***Eat*** breakfast or bring a snack to eat at the break.

- ***Follow directions*** exactly and ask questions if you need clarification.

- Mark your answer folder *carefully* and fill in the ovals neatly.

- Don't spend too much *time* on any single question. For hard ones, *choose the answer* you think is best and move on.

Imp ✓ • Just like the ACT, there is *no penalty for guessing*. Be sure to answer every question.

PSAT

Imp The PSAT is a rite of passage for high school sophomores and juniors. For sophomores, it is a practice test that *parallels the SAT I*. There are a few differences in the PSAT and the SAT I. It is important to know this to perform more efficiently on the PSAT. *Colleges do not see the PSAT scores for admissions purposes. It's only practical!* The "P" in PSAT means "preliminary." What this means to the student is the opportunity to *practice* on this one test day.

SAT II

Check to see if there are colleges you are thinking about that require the SAT II Subject Tests. *Most selective colleges require three. These tests are used to verify information given by your high school to balance ranking, grades and teacher recommendation statements*. Begin to prepare for one or two of the SAT II tests for subjects in which you excel. If so, take one or more after completing a high school course in them, usually *the May or June testing period*. You can take a total of three in one morning (they are only one hour tests for each subject) if your stamina will allow you to do your best on all three. If not, just take one or two per session. You can check online or in the back of a college handbook for *college requirements* for this test.

CHAPTER 4

11ᵗʰ Grade: GPA Finale

Transcript

The junior year of high school is usually very challenging academically as well as tense, since it is the first time students realize that they will seriously begin to plan where they will be for the four years following graduation. It is a big year for testing! *It is the last year to work toward a transcript that speaks of a good course selection as well as a competitive GPA. It is in this final year that the transcript will be completed for applying to many of your colleges.*

Timeline

August – December

Scholarships: Check for scholarships that are posted on the high school website and in a scholarship bulletin, if your school counselor's office prints one (usually once a month). Check for ones you may qualify for now, as well as ones you may qualify for in your senior year.

PSAT: The high school (*Student Bulletin* containing valuable test-taking tips and a practice test is given to students by the counselor) will schedule the taking of the PSAT as set by the College Board. It is usually in the month of October. During the junior year, students can compete in the *National Merit Scholarship Program*. The *Selection Index Number* is what determines whether a student makes the cut for the National Merit Semi-Finalists. The Selection Index number is a sum of two categories on the PSAT test *Critical Reading and Math*. The Selection Index Number is set by the sum of all the students in a given state that take the test. For example, if *you* live in Tennessee, the numbers that determine the Selection Index Number are taken from the students that take the PSAT in that state only. *A student* is not competing with students from any other state.

If a student becomes a *National Merit Semi-Finalist* (notified during the senior year), as a competition requirement, the student must take the *SAT I* or can retake it to improve scores. There is an important form with an *essay portion* for the *student* to fill out and the *high school counselor* to return by the deadline. The student will then be competing for the *National Merit Finalists*. Some students won't make the cut for the semi-finalist, but who may qualify for *Commended*. All of these awards raise the probability for admittance into colleges and universities. In the case of the finalists, money awards are possible, about *$2,000*, for the student, with some colleges offering merit scholarships/financial aid and other amenities to entice that student to attend their school.

In other words, the results can make you more marketable to colleges and universities.

TIP: *The PSAT/NMSQT* **penalizes students for guessing** *by subtracting a fraction of a point from their score for every incorrect response. If a student has no idea of the answer, leave it blank. If the student can eliminate one or more answers, make an* **"educated guess."** **Practice tests** *help you budget your time better during each "timed section."*

In December, students will receive the PSAT results. **Students** should analyze their level of performance and—in order to better prepare for the SAT I—compare their test and answer sheet with a friend who did well on the test and learn what **they** don't know now.

Resumé Development: Continue adding and revising your resumé Identify a **theme** for your talents and/or abilities and begin to **add other activities which apply**.

College Fairs: Attend local college fairs (usually in the fall). Information is posted through the counselor's office on high school bulletin boards and in local publications. Prior to going, look over the list of schools represented and identify the ones you would like to speak with (schools are usually set up in alphabetical order). **Ask questions** that include academics, sports, support services, financial aid, scholarships, etc. Collect the materials offered to you. **(Bring a bag to hold them.)** Using the addresses on the cards you collected, **write a note** to that college's counselor if you are extremely interested in that school. This connection with a prospective school counselor's office will help as you get further along in the admissions process.

College Representatives: During the fall, most college representatives will schedule a time to meet with students in each high school. The counselor should post those days and times. Look up the college online prior to meeting with the representative. This will help you prepare smart questions to ask. Make sure you ask for his/her card and introduce yourself. **This representative could very well be the one who reads your application.**

Test Prep Courses: Research ways to sign up for **SAT I and/or ACT prep classes or sessions** offered by your high school or a local university or private source. The hints you receive will help. However, it is important to weigh the cost against the value of your particular situation. Many courses like the **Princeton Review and Kaplan Course** (approximately a six week commitment once a week) take time and you are one of many in a room. If your time is tight and you perform better in a smaller group, or even a one on one situation, then you might think about a ***private student session or an adult tutor*** or a short-term session. Learning centers also offer courses, but once again, it is a time and money matter that you must weigh.

Financial Aid Workshops: These are sometimes offered by the high school as well as at college and career nights. Parents are the main attendees, but students can benefit by understanding what they can do to add to the promise of possible aid.

January – May

Junior Conference: Counselors, in smaller schools (mainly private) will schedule a junior conference for the student and parent(s) to attend. At this conference, the counselor will have the transcript and any scores (PLAN /PSAT) available. The student should ***bring his/her resumé*** and a list of ***colleges they're interested in***. The purpose of the conference is to discuss colleges that are appropriate for the student as a starting point for the college search.

Course selection: Make sure the courses ***you*** choose will meet all requirements for graduation. Colleges may request a Mid-Year report. This is delivered by the counselor, after the first semester senior year, and includes ***the student's*** transcript to the schools that request it. (Keep up those grades; it does matter, even if ***you*** have been accepted. ***A decline in grades can prompt a school to withdraw the invitation to the student to attend in the fall.***

Scholarship Search: Even though juniors will apply for many scholarships in the fall of their senior year, you should start looking at scholarship possibilities early in the high school years.

Testing

ACT/SAT I

The standardized tests dates can be found online (SAT I/II at **www.collegeboard.com** and the ACT at **www.act.org**), and are posted in the counselor's office. Also, **practice booklets** are available in the counselor's office for both tests.

Register to have the **scores sent to the colleges** to which you plan to apply. It is free up to four or five schools. There is a per-school fee above this level. ACT/SAT I only sends **one score per test period**, so as you take more tests, make sure you request these scores from an additional test period to be sent to your college choices.

May is the most popular month for taking the **SAT I** and June is the most popular month for taking the **ACT**. **Sign up for these tests in January or February.** Otherwise you may have to go on standby and/or you may have to travel some distance if the most desirable and closest sites fill early.

SAT II

In the early spring buy **SAT II practice booklets** and prepare to take SAT II tests when you complete a subject or two at the end of the year. (Test dates are found online at **www.collegeboard.com**). Sign up early to insure a spot at your preferred testing site. Three one-hour tests can be taken at each testing date.

Myth

"If I Send All My Scores and Some Are Not That High, It Can Be A Negative" On the contrary. Some schools will "super score" (taking the best score for each section—Math, Critical Reading, Writing—from multiple retakes and combining them, rather than just taking scores from one sitting) the SAT I by choosing the highest number from any given subtest scores and recalculating a new composite. Some schools are beginning to work the ACT scores in this same manner.

SAT I and ACT Preparation Guides

  – *The Real ACT Prep Guide*

  – *Official Guide to the ACT Assessment*

  – *Cracking the ACT/ Princeton Review*

  – *8 Real SATs/ College Board*

  – *Up Your Score (SAT)/ Workman Publishing*

What to Think About While Taking the SAT I

Remember that there are no hidden meanings.

According to The College Board, the Critical Reading portion of the SAT I has two types of questions: sentence completion, which is relatively simple and some vocabulary. The passage-based questions test your ability to comprehend, analyze, and even evaluate reading passages. The reading level is not high, but the questions can seem vague and ambiguous. The important thing to remember is that the passage holds the answers to the questions. Even difficult vocabulary may be defined in the passage, as well. It is best to work backwards-forwards in that you should read the questions before reading the passage to understand what you are looking for in the paragraph.

The Math section presents both multiply choice and "grid-in" questions. The basic rules of algebra and geometry will be used to answer the questions. For problem solving questions, SAT arranges them in ascending order of difficulty, which means you should not spend too much time on the first questions, since they are the easiest. Look at key question words like *"not"* and *"except"*. If you are not readily sure of how to work the problem, start with "C," the median value of the answer choices. If your answer is greater than "C," then you know the answer is probably "A" or "B." If the answer you yield is smaller than "C" then the answer is probably "D" or "E." For the grid section, always check your math before gridding.

College Visits

Visit Colleges/Universities

Visit the schools that interest you. Consider money and time when deciding to travel (spring break or summer). You can wait and see if you are accepted and then visit. One bit of advice: Find out if **showing interest** is a plus at that school (call their admissions office). If it is, be sure to schedule a visit if time/money allows. Make sure the school is currently in session-not on spring break- so you are able to see and speak with students. If that timing doesn't work out, you can visit in June or July and will at least see some students that attend summer classes. Also, if you are interested in a college, you can schedule **an interview (usually not formal), or a meeting with a counselor** when you visit. **If you decide to choose Early Decision or Early Action when applying, you will have seen some colleges to help you decide your method of applying in the fall.**

College Tours

Sign up to take the high school sponsored college tour, even if the schools to visit are not your choices. The experience of seeing campuses of different sizes will help narrow your search.

Tips for a Terrific College Visit

Do:

- Record your observations.

- Talk to students on every campus.

- Follow your visit up with a thank you note, if you personally met with anyone (Admission Counselor, Dean of a college, coach, etc.

- Analyze the school as a whole.

- Take photographs.

- Read copies of the school newspaper.

- Look at the bulletin boards and other postings for activities that interest you.

- Roam the campus by yourself and get the feel of whether it fits you.

- Walk or drive around the community surrounding the college.

- Eat a meal somewhere on campus.

- Go to the student activities center or office. Find out which activities freshmen can join and if one particular activity dominates such as Greek letter organizations, sports, the local bar scene, etc.

- Check the public transportation (on and off campus).

- Ask about safety and crime issues.

- Ask where freshmen live.

Don't:

- Evaluate the school on the basis of a visit there by someone you know, even if you visit together.

- Judge the school solely on the impressions of your tour guide.

- Let the weather on the day of your visit totally influence your impression.

- Make snap judgments.

- Let perceived quality or academic reputation totally affect you. Your task is to find the right colleges for you.

• Judge the school solely on impressions made on your visit. Remember what you have read and heard about the college before your visit.

College Search

Consider the parameters of your interest, needs and abilities when making a college list. Such as the following:

1. Size of physical campus

2. Regional location

3. Town/city (large or small)

4. Student population

5. Distance from home

6. Weather

7. Majors offered

8. Reputation of the school or programs

9. Competitiveness

10. Cost (discussion should be between parents and student)

11. Facilities

12. Types of institutions (large, medium, or small in population, two year vs four year, religious, private, public, Ivy League, art, music, conservatory, women's, men's, technical, etc.)

TIP: *Once you have identified colleges, request to be put on the admissions office emailing list. You will then be able to receive information about visitation days and upcoming events.*

Book Sources to Use

– *The College Handbook by College Board*

– *The Best Colleges by Princeton Review*

– *The Fisk Guide to Colleges by Edward B. Fisk*

– *Rugg's Recommendations on the Colleges by Frederick Rugg*

– *Barron's Top 50: An inside Look at America's Best Colleges by Fischgrund*

– *The Gourman Report by Jack Gourman*

– *Peterson's Competitive Colleges/ Petersons*

– *Peterson's Guide to Four-Year Colleges/Petersons*

– *Peterson's 440 Great Colleges for Top Students/Petersons*

The Spring and Summer Prior to the Senior Year

• Research summer internships and enrichment activities (ones that will help you grow and learn more about an area you have already participated in).

• Begin researching private scholarship resources; identify specific criteria and mark deadlines.

• Attend additional college fairs and on-campus activities.

• Attend financial aid information sessions (parents and students).

• Plan to visit colleges.

• Sign up to take SAT I/SAT II and/or ACT.

• Consider enrolling in an academic course at a local university during the summer.

- Develop a college list of preferred schools (two "sure bets", two "middle of the road", and two "reaches").

- Review specific admissions/scholarship criteria.

- Develop college time lines (include dates for tests, applications deadlines, financial aid applications, etc.).

- Discuss college plans with your parents.

- Begin working on college essays (many applications are available online in July).

- Fill out the Common Application (Online August 1 as of 2010).

- Decide which colleges you will apply Early Action, Regular Decision and if appropriate, Early Decision.

- In August, sign up for fall standardized testing.

Advice From Seniors to Rising Juniors

1. It is harder to raise your GPA in the junior year than you think it will be.

2. Start looking at colleges in the spring of your junior year.

3. Campus visits can help you narrow your list down.

4. Make sure colleges offer a good environment for you.

5. Ask about the negatives when you visit a college.

6. Like your back-up schools—you may need them.

7. Don't pick a school just because your friends like it or are going there.

8. Don't get hooked on just one school—you might not end up going there.

9. Don't obsess about the college process—you still need to do well in school.

10. Think about jobs and community service during the summer.

11. Form good relationships with some teachers—you will need recommendations.

12. If you will be submitting an art portfolio, speak with your art teacher about how to collect your work and arrange all of your items according to the directions instructed in the portfolio packet.

13. If the military is your choice or a military academy, start getting recommendations in the spring of the junior year.

14. Look at applications now to see what they entail, including essays and short answers.

15. Start your essays in the summer.

16. Plan taking your SAT I and SAT II (if required) so you can fit them all in.

17. Prepare for standardized testing.

18. Prepare a resumé to be added to as the junior year and senior year progresses.

19. Don't choose a school based on its football team.

CHAPTER 5

12th Grade: The Application Process

Summer Before the Senior Year

- *During the summer of your rising (which means pre) senior year, fill out applications* (college forms or common application) and work on *essays* and *short answers*.

- Check each college for *online applications*. Some applications may be placed online for the next fall year as early as June and others as late as September.

- Sign up online for *SAT I* and/or *ACT* test dates. Register scores to be sent to your choice colleges. Send in any *SAT II and AP test results* that have not been sent to the student's college choices. *Keep up your grades for the year! (Your college of choice has the right to take back a student's invitation to attend when it receives the final transcript).*

- *Common Application:* The Common Application is an undergraduate college admission application that applicants can use to apply to any of the 392 member colleges and universities in the U.S. It streamlines the college application process for students choosing to apply to those colleges. That way, a student only fills out demographics once and that information is distributed to the member institutions that the student chooses. These institutions may choose an additional supplement form for students to submit which may include essays and/or short answers. If a college offers both the Common Application and their own form, it is advisable to *use their own application* to show interest in the extra time it takes to obtain their application. Most college's websites will have a *PDF form to download*. The Common Application can be found at www.commonapp.org and usually becomes available online the beginning of August. If the Common Application is used, there are supplements for many schools requiring essays and short answers. Check the specific college web page for these supplements.

Fall of the Senior Year

September – December

- Start preparing for taking the SAT I/ SAT II and/or ACT.

- Utilize Internet resources to find additional information about colleges and programs.

- Attend one or two open houses at local campuses.

- Fill out Rolling Admission applications to colleges and send them in early fall.

- *STUDY!*

- Check your high school's schedule for conferences with **college representatives**.

- Attend **college fairs**.

- Be aware of any **scholarship opportunities** through your high school, private and public ones.

- Write **essays for long and short questions** requested on application forms.

- Finalize your **resumé** (update it from the summer and add any activities that will take place during your senior year). Give a copy to your counselor. Make a **list of these activities by order of interests** to be used on college applications.

- Finalize a **college list** and begin to **fill out applications**.

- Applications have many parts: The **application, mid-year report, teacher recommendation forms, school report form**, etc. Give the counselor the school report form and the mid-year report form along with **your** requests of which colleges to send in **his/her** portion (**your** official transcript, school profile, **your** resumé, and **his/her** school report form.)

- Decide about applying **Early Action, Early Decision or Regular Decision and note deadlines of each**.

- Request **letters of recommendation** from teachers and/or others. (Instructions included in chapter 13).

- Meet with your counselor to discuss your theme and how it should be mentioned in his/her recommendation—meet with the teachers who agree to give you recommendations about this as well.

- Ask your counselor to write to college admission officers for **fee waivers** if you cannot afford to pay the **application fees**.

- Keep a **folder** of information for each college.

- Make *copies* of all applications sent.

- Check requests and dates of the schools that require the CSS Profile, a form that allows students to apply for financial aid. It is more detailed than the FAFSA and allows private member institutions of the College Board to look into the finances of a student and family in a more detailed way. Unlike the FAFSA, that is free, the CSS Profile does charge a fee, varying from year to year. This form can be found online of private colleges and universities that require it. Also, check for any *college specific financial aid form* required by that specific college.

- Research *college scholarship applications*, determine whether or not your application for admissions is automatically as an application used for scholarships

- *Visit colleges* that may be priority schools on your list.

- Double *check with your counselor* to ensure that he/she has *sent in all materials* you requested in the application process.

- Check with any *person sending a recommendation* for you to ensure that they have mailed it or given it to the counselor to mail.

- If Early Decision or Early Action is chosen, check online at those specific colleges to make sure the materials were received. If some are lacking, respond immediately.

Mid-Year of the Senior Year

January – April

- Complete the *FAFSA* form (as close to the beginning of the year as possible—you can estimate your financial returns) and submit online.

- Contact your counselor to make sure that he/she has mailed your *mid-year report* to each of the schools that requested it.

- Colleges offering you an invitation for a scholarship possibility will send a letter inviting you to a **special day** at which time you will be **interviewed** to compete for that particular scholarship.

- **Revisit or visit** schools from which you have received an acceptance letter..

- If accepted, **fill out the housing form**, even if you have not committed to that particular school.

- Watch for **financial aid awards** that will be mailed.

Month of May

- Notify the college of your **choice** as well as scholarships on **MAY 1.** **Students Rights and Responsibilities specify that a student has until May 1 to answer a college of his/her acceptance of attendance or scholarship acceptance. Any college requesting a student's commitment before May 1 is violating this rule and needs a call from the counselor.**

- **Notify other colleges** that offered you admission. Kindly e-mail or write them that you appreciate the invitation to attend, but you have decided to attend another college.

- Many high school counseling offices will send your final transcript to your college of choice along with verification of your graduation date. **Make sure that you have told your counselor which college you have chosen.**

- **Wait listed**—if you are put on a wait list, and you really want that school, notify the school by returning their form that states that you are still interested. Any additional information (change in better grades with a letter of explanation, a special recommendation that explains why you are a candidate for that school) that can be sent to the college is helpful.

- If you can wait for their decision (sometimes by June 1 or later, then you can *say "YES" to another school on May 1*.

- If you are offered an invitation from the *wait-listed school*, you can say *"YES" to them. Then notify the previous committed school and say, "I appreciate the invitation to attend your college, but I just received an invitation from another school where I had been wait listed and have decided to attend that school."*

- Take *AP tests*, if appropriate.

Summer Months After the Senior Year

June

- Your college of choice will send you information about orientation dates, housing (if you have not already sent it in), roommate notification, etc.

- Courses that are transferable to your college can be taken at a local college or university.

- Working during the summer can help with extra money needed during your freshman year.

- Your high school will send your final report, which includes your transcript and date of graduation.

- Enjoy your family. When you leave to begin school home will become a special place to visit.

July

- Speaking with your roommate allows you to get to know a little bit about each other, maybe make decorating plans, etc.

- Start accumulating things to take to college that will be necessary, useful and help you feel at home.

August

- Make a list of your friends' e-mail addresses, so you will be able to exchange street addresses once you're settled in your new college.

- Make a list of items that you will buy once you arrive in your new college town or city (there is no sense in packing every toiletry or item, when much can be purchased once you arrive).

- If you are going out for "Sorority Rush" plan your attire for each day (most schools will tell you what to expect for "Rush Week").

- Once you arrive on campus and have your schedule, check out the buildings where your classes will be held.

CHAPTER 6

Molding the Student Through the College Planning Process

When students reach high school, there are areas of improvement to be addressed to make the adjustment to college life easier. It is important to understand how grades nine through twelve can be a time of learning life skills while preparing for college.

While working with students and trying to match colleges that profiled their numbers (grades and scores) as well as their core curriculum, their interests, abilities and willingness to compete academically, I realized that all of these factors would be listed on a page as a formula to provide a list of colleges to work with during the application process. But I needed to go a step further. Knowing that high school years are filled with confusion (elation, mood swings, fights with parents, resentment of authority, experimentation with sex, drugs, alcohol, dating and relationships, and self-discovery) I began working with students to help them use this college process to improve themselves and their choices through awareness and implementation.

The continuation of molding students through this process and working on their weaknesses academically and personally, as well as teaching them life skills was my opportunity to better prepare them for the college years.

There are many examples of how this should and can be done, and is a process in which students begin to not only know themselves better, but admit to themselves that they need to improve on their weaknesses and expand on their strengths. *Self-improvement* becomes the focus for the student because it is vital to improve your weaknesses that could negatively affect your application and scholarship deadlines. It is important to improve your strengths which may encourage you to "go outside the box" with one of your interests and therefore affect your application in a positive way. While this is the first step, it always elevates to the next level, which is: what can be done to improve the student's weaknesses and develop his/her strengths? Parents are often concerned about losing control during the high school years. Teenagers, for the most part, are very private and will hide any faults, mistakes, thoughts, experiences or weaknesses from their parents, if possible. This is a part of the phase in which students are not only pulling away from parents, but also mistakenly feeling they are independent because of it. The reality is that students are actually dependent on their weaknesses such as being a procrastinator, but they seem at times to succeed in spite of this flaw. This becomes their norm and they learn to live with this style. It begins, in some cases, to be accepted by their peers, and even parents and teachers. At this age, it is important to have something like getting into their college of choice to help them realize that they need to improve upon bad habits that will negatively affect the application process and their success in college. *The college planning process is a great way to have students develop and improve personally, such as learning responsibility.*

The students I have worked with come from homes with various family dynamics; some very supportive, some with only one parent involved, some with fairly good relationships with their parents and some not, some with well established goals of which colleges to attend and some with no idea. Organized students and procrastinators. Arrogant students and shy ones. No matter how different each student I worked with was, they all thought they could depend on what they saw as their strong traits. They rarely allowed their negative traits to surface or were unaware they existed. If a student made an A in English, but had trouble writing a paragraph for a college essay question, he/she was not concerned. Unfortunately, many times a grade was thought to be the only measure of success.

I used the college process to help the student take a "holistic approach" —one that addressed the fact that we, as people, are multi-faceted. Every student needs to experience personal growth and development through their involvement in the college planning process.

As I began to look at the competition of today's college admissions, I realized one important factor that is a must for being admitted and winning scholarships. Beyond numbers (GPA and standardized test scores), the ***most important factor in the application process is character and personal development***. I then knew that it was vital to have students look at their character in terms of traits (commitment, dedication, caring, promptness, being responsible, developing personal talents, setting and reaching goals, etc.) and emphasize these during the college application process.

A Few Examples:

Math Strength

One of my students was proficient in Math. I contacted a local agency that had classes for unwed teenage mothers who had dropped out of high school. The student, the director and I met to discuss how this student could work with this program. The student created a curriculum to teach basic Math to help the young mothers pass their GED. The student and I then spoke with his high school to plan his course schedule so that twice a week he would be able to teach at the center during a free period and lunch. During the application process, the director of the center sent a recommendation noting the student's character and the work he had done there. This student not only was *accepted at University of Virginia and University of North Carolina at Chapel Hill, but he was offered a full financial ride to both*.

Sports Strength

There was a girl who wanted to specialize in personal development in sports. I contacted a special needs school and we met with the principal about setting up a program. Working with the coach there, this student developed a set program to help Autistic children learn to catch a ball, kick a ball, play as a team member, etc. In addition, the student developed a guide for parents that included how to implement these skills for their special children. *This student was admitted into the University of Richmond.*

Music Strength

Another student I had was proficient in piano. I contacted a local assisted living facility and asked about the Alzheimer residents. The director was able to coordinate this student to come and play the piano for Alzheimer individuals. Because certain classical music is stimulating to the brain, this student chose pieces that would be most effective for these individuals. *She was accepted by Furman University, Wake Forest University and David Lipscomb University. She was offered substantial scholarship money from the first two colleges and a full ride to Lipscomb University, which she attended.*

Science Strength

One student was interested in science. Her grandmother had Parkinson's disease. I recommended that she contact a research professor at New York University, who was researching the disease. (Her Mother taught there and they lived in Manhattan.) The student was able to help this professor with his research and was accepted at *Washington University*.

Language Strength

A student who knew the Spanish language well was vice-president of the Spanish Club in his high school. He had also built doll houses to put in an abused children's shelter waiting room. He mentioned that there were no other toys for the children while the parent was being interviewed and they were being settled. As in most areas in the United States, there are Spanish speaking families as well as Caucasian families that need this kind of refuge. I suggested that he use his man power within the Spanish Club to collect books, both in Spanish and English and start a library of books for the children's waiting room. In addition, I suggested that he publish a book with both English and Spanish words under pictures to teach both languages to children. Both entertaining and educational books would help these temporarily housed children, who had to leave in a hurry with a parent to escape domestic abuse. This student is a junior in high school, but hopes to apply to competitive schools.

Community Service Strength

One student I was able to help had always been interested in community service projects. He volunteered at a community center where underprivileged children attended. As he helped the children, he took a specific interest in a girl who seemed to need more help than the others. Her self-esteem was low and she had been expelled from one school and was attempting to do better in another. This student realized that the child's home life was less than supportive and in fact, disruptive for her. He began to help her with her studies and even challenged her to succeed where she was weak - he promised to do the same in his own life. Needless to say, she began to succeed in school and received good grades. I encouraged this student to write about this in his application essay. He was awarded an invitation to attend *Haverford College*.

Developing a Theme

It is very important to work on the following areas to show consistency in your application:

- Specific area of study

- The essay

- A teacher recommendation

- A counselor recommendation

- A special person recommendation (such as a director of a program in which you participated).

- A special project or community service

EXAMPLE: History Theme

Specific Area of Study:

A student chose History as his favorite subject. He was also President of the Student Body Association in his high school. Considering these two points, he read about leaders in history that he admired and then planned the implementation of the qualities of these leaders through his leadership position of the SGA (Student Government Association).

The Essay:

By expressing his involvement and implementation of qualities and ideas taken from his academic interest in leaders of history, he was able to write an essay showing his development as a student, and his interest in using historical figures as role models to help develop his own leadership qualities and to help implement productive programs.

A Teacher Recommendation:

Choosing a History teacher to write his recommendation, he planned his strategy. He not only participated in class, but periodically brought in extra articles that enhanced the teacher's lectures. By going outside the box in the high school classroom, he was able to present himself as an intellectually interested student, which came to light during the application process. When he asked this teacher to write a recommendation, he asked him to please reflect upon his efforts and interest, his work ethic and participation in class. Colleges want to know what kind of student you will be in the college classroom and therefore put a great deal of weight on a recommendation that reflects this.

The Counselor Recommendation:

This student got to know his counselor prior to the senior year. Counselors get much of their information from forms distributed to the student's teachers as well as being aware of a student's school participation. This student spoke to the counselor and suggested specific teachers for her to gather his personal information in order to help keep the theme consistent.

A Special Project or Community Service:

As President of the SGA, this student planned a forum where the candidates for Governor of his state would be invited to address the student body. His purpose was to create awareness and interest for students, who are the future voters. This project addressed his interest in the political agendas of different periods in history, and extended it to a student body, which helped make history.

Presenting yourself in a consistent manner (through essays, teacher recommendations, counselor recommendations, etc.) gives the college counselor reading your application an understanding of who you are. This is the key to a better chance of acceptance into the colleges of your choice. You're GPA and standardized scores just put you in line for competing. It is your consistent theme shown through your essay, specific area of study, a related community service or special project and a teacher's/ counselor's or directors recommendation that reflects how you operate in the classroom, your qualities of a good work ethic, intellectual curiosity and a giving and caring character. All of these things will ensure you a better chance of acceptance by a college.

Awareness is the Beginning, Involvement is the Teacher

Many high schools, religious youth groups, clubs and organizations will offer or require a community service day or week project. This will grow the student's awareness of community needs, which is good, but leaves out an important factor; the student's *long term focus and commitment* to something or someone else.

Skill Learning

One student I worked with was extremely shy. She only gave answers in one or two word sentences and was very unsure of herself. She did express an interest in majoring in business. I knew that she would need to be able to express her thoughts and plans more thoroughly. She was very bright academically, but did not perform up to her potential. Her parents were concerned about her speaking to others in a very low voice and that her comments went unheard. Waiting for her to mature and develop this skill would set her back in the high school experience and readiness for college. "Late bloomers" either socially or academically do not achieve well enough to keep up with their peers. This can result in low self-esteem. This can be avoided by *using the college planning process as a guide to learning these skills*. Parents should use the services of a school or independent counselor for help during this period of development. The following twelve steps can help the student correct weaknesses by:

1. The student practicing in mock interviews.

2. The counselor organizing social situations (teaching the student how to address another adult and then having another adult enter the room for practice),

3. The counselor getting a student or adult tutor to help with weak subjects.

4. The student using the results of the ACT, SAT I, and PSAT *Imp* (returned test booklet of the PSAT and the ordered test from ACT/SAT) to check academic weaknesses (have the student rework wrong answers with a teacher or tutor).

5. The parent or counselor coordinating the students interests, abilities and skills.

6. The parent or counselor requiring the student to use a calendar to become better organized.

7. The counselor requiring the student to follow a timeline in preparation for the application process.

8. The parent giving the student the responsibility to research colleges and to contact the counselor with the information found.

9. The counselor discussing with the student how to live with parents during the teenage years and what responsibilities they must take in order to have the independence they want.

10. The counselor helping the student become aware of community needs, and learning to become a part of their environment and other groups.

11. The counselor should help students become less egotistical and more realistic about themselves.

12. The counselor and parent, most of all during this process, should help students learn who they are at this moment in time.

By improving and understanding themselves, students can portray their character on a college application.

Let's look at what is happening to the student during the beginning of the college search process:

- The student is forced to consider financial restraints when looking at colleges.

- The student is limited by his/her level of accomplishments when looking at schools.

- The student has the opportunity to look at competitive colleges due to their high accomplishments.

- The student is beginning to hear about colleges that friends are considering.

- The student is beginning to tolerate the parents questioning him/her about his/her future college plans.

- The student is beginning to understand the necessity of college visits.

- The student is given the opportunity to meet with college representatives that visit the high school.

- The student attends the junior conference, scheduled by the counselor, with parents present to discuss future college plans.

- The student fills out private scholarship forms in hopes to win some money for college.

- The student is faced with the reality of making decisions between attending the same college as high school friends or deciding to be a new kid on the block.

- The student is quite often asked by others, "So what college are you going to go to?"

The most important person that needs to deal with all these issues is the student. If the student is pro-active in the process, then parents can breathe a sigh of relief. In most cases, the student is completely engrossed in trying to pass the eleventh grade, deal with friendships and satisfy the demands of activities outside the classroom. Therefore, planning a thorough college search is either put on the back burner or dealt with in a casual way. This creates frustration for the parents, who, in general, the student would rather not have to answer to. Then the battle begins. If the parents have attended college, it has been awhile and the process and competition has changed. If the parents did not attend college, the process is totally foreign to them. In either case, the parents need the time, patience, and knowledge to help in this process.

The student must have some *guidance* to sort out this enormous task that includes choosing the schools that fit them academically, location wise, weather wise, size wise, program wise and implement the application process successfully. Books and online information is readily available to the student to become familiar with each school, but the information can be confusing to sort out. Also, the strategy to use in order to compete for admissions and scholarships can be difficult to determine. This is the hardest task, since it takes investigation and a follow through on the part of an adult to help them tap resources.

Let's look at how your student can mature and develop life skills while going through the college admissions process.

The first order of business is for the parent to objectively list the strengths and weaknesses of their son/daughter.

For Example:

- Her strengths lie in English and History, but she is not as strong in the areas of Math and Science.

- She is a good writer, but lacks the experience in creative writing.

- She is involved in high school sports and drama, but is not the best on the team or in the group.

- She has never had a job.

- She procrastinates on schoolwork and deadlines and forgets to use a calendar, but is smart enough to pull it off.

- She is outgoing, but underneath she feels incompetent to deal with her weaknesses.

Let's create a scenario to help her prepare for the college admissions process:

Sarah is a sophomore in high school. She has around a 3.8 GPA on a 4.0 scale and is signed up to take the PSAT and the PLAN test in a couple of months. She is presently taking AP European History, Honors English, Algebra II with Trigonometry, and Biology. Sarah needs to prioritize and deal with her weaknesses. The first step would be to help her organize and check her calendar regularly. Find a mentor to help her with this step.

How do you find this person?

- Have Sarah get a job and share with the boss what she needs in terms of expectations to be on time, and promptly do her job.

- Have her volunteer for a community service organization or church/synagogue youth group. Ask the adult leader to help you out by placing Sarah in a position of responsibility and demanding excellence from her.

- Connect Sarah with an upperclassman who can get her involved in a school related project and be her mentor. Be careful not to portray Sarah as a needy person. It is important to talk with this upperclassman about what you'd like Sarah to experience in order to help her learn and mature.

The impact for Sarah:

- A mentor for her

- Involvement in activities outside of class

- Possible leadership opportunities

- Learning from an experienced peer

- Learning to work with another adult

- Earning money

- Taking on responsibility

- Learning to balance a job, school, volunteer work, etc.

- Depending on what project Sarah selects, it can show her passion and /or a love of learning

At the same time, Sarah is exhibiting attractive traits that colleges covet by showing she has developed a character of hard work, a high level of initiative, a time commitment outside of class, and a passion/love for learning. ***ALL OF THESE QUALITIES ARE WHAT COMPETITIVE COLLEGES AND SCHOLARSHIP COMMITTEES ARE LOOKING FOR IN THEIR APPLICANTS!***

Student Learning During the College Application Process

As parents of a high school student who will be leaving home in a short few years, it is realistic to want to fix your student's major weaknesses and teach life skills that you know will be needed later in life. ***THE COLLEGE PLANNING PROCESS IS WHERE THIS CAN HAPPEN!*** Your student can benefit from this process in many ways:

- Learning to make important life altering decisions.

- Learning to acknowledge weaknesses.

- Learning to acknowledge strengths.

- Learning to keep good records of transactions.

- Learning to think outside the box.

- Learning to use existing talents to develop leadership.

- Learning to work with a counselor.

- Learning to research.

- Learning to follow through.

- Learning to meet deadlines.

- Learning to work with parents toward a common goal.

- Learning to co-ordinate between teachers, counselors and parents.

- Learning new self-awareness.

Learning to Make Important Life Altering Decisions

Previously, the decision to enroll your student in school was made by you, the parents. This time, it will be mostly the student's decision. This will, in most cases, be the first big decision that your student will make for himself/herself. Because of these concerns, it is important that your student have some guidance outside the family to help learn how to make a decision of this magnitude. If there is a *school counselor* that can help, utilize his/her services. Many school counselors are overloaded with large numbers of students and other duties and do not have the time to work with a student one-on-one. Engaging an *independent counselor* could be your solution.

Learning to Acknowledge Weaknesses

This is a very difficult area. Self-improvement through acknowledging and tackling weaknesses is not a challenge a growing teenager wants to waste their time on. In fact, a famous line from a teenager is, "This is the way I am. Accept it. I can't change." This can make a parent feel a loss of control, since there is no cooperation on the part of their student. Then there is the frustrated parent, who has lived with their student's weaknesses that don't seem to go away. Often parents punish their students and set rules. Other parents try to have reasonable conversations with their student about working on weaknesses. Though these approaches might work at first, they usually have a short shelf life. As a result, the student continues to struggle with these weaknesses.

Since the counselor doesn't have the emotional attachment to the student that the family does, the student is more likely to open up to the counselor about his/her weaknesses and how to work on them. The counselor can really help to set the student up to improve weaknesses and therefore eliminate these negatives before going to college. The choice of a counselor has to be one that has the time to do this. As mentioned before, many school counselors are limited in their time with students when dealing with the college application process. ***Independent counselors*** use their time in this capacity.

Learning to Acknowledge Strengths

Many students recognize what they do best. This is easy. However, knowing how to play up these strengths for college preparation isn't always obvious. It is important for a parent and/or counselor to help students utilize their strong points by suggesting ways to use them. In a short word for parents, it is called "molding". For the counselor, it's called "developing". The end result is the same in that the student goes beyond the obvious to improve their strongest assets.

Learning to Keep Good Records of College Transactions

A student should have a notebook with each college separated by section. Each section should contain a list of deadlines, a copy of all application information sent, and scholarship possibilities. Mailings received from colleges should also be placed in the section as well as students notes when researching.

Learning To Think Outside the Box

Students know what they are good at and what their interests are. The only problem is that they always see themselves as the sole participator. By going outside the box, they bring others into their special area of interests. For example, I had a high school student who was interested in government and politics. He was involved in an organization called Youth Legislature, in which he not only learned about government, but practiced-participated, appropriate to his age. He decided to extend his knowledge to middle school students by planning and holding seminars at his school to teach awareness and facts about government. His goal was to encourage students to get involved in the youth legislature program. His long- term goal was to create an interest in government among students he saw as future voters. This category is one of the extras that colleges are looking for.

Learning to Use Talents to Develop Leadership

Students can be leaders in many ways, large and small. I had a student who loved to bake and cook. She decided to learn about nutrition for herself and through the process learned that many children did not eat healthily. She then decided to hold cooking classes where she incorporated knowledge about good food choices. By doing this, she showed leadership and helped young children at the same time. This is impressive to colleges because it not only shows initiative and caring, but that she is creative.

Learning to Work With a Counselor

Students will have to work with a counselor in college and in many cases one that they will not know. In order to gain some experience in how to communicate with a counselor, the student can take this opportunity in high school through the college application process. The student can do this in the following ways with their high school counselor:

- Make a *list of colleges* to ask the counselor about.

- Make an *appointment* with the counselor and *be on time*.

- Take a *note pad* to write down any instructions the counselor gives.

- Discuss your *goals and interests*, so the counselor can make specific suggestions of colleges to research.

- Bring the *correct forms* to the counselor in a *timely manner*, so as to give him/her plenty of time to fill them out.

- Bring your rough draft of the *essay* for the counselor to critique.

- Ask about any *scholarship opportunities* and follow through with deadlines.

- In general, take the *responsibility of a timeline* and work with the counselor using his/her *knowledge and advice* for applying to college.

Learning to Research

A student should approach research with the mind set of "shopping around." In that respect, students should be wary of choosing colleges that represent extremes, with nothing in-between (local university or Ivy-League). To research a college, a student should:

- Look in college books, like The College Board Handbook, for statistics about college profiles (also online).

- Make a list of states that are an acceptable distance from home (getting home in a day or paying for air flight), weather, work or internship opportunities, family close by, etc.

- Know *your* scores and GPA and compare to schools listings to determine two reach schools, two realistic, and two sure-bets.

- Keep listings of the statistics of each school: the population, SAT/ACT and GPA requirements, SAT II requirements, high school graduation requirements, the majors you are interested in, athletics, diversity in the student population, Greek system, percentage that live on campus, cost to attend, special student services, if applicable, and contact information.

- Take online virtual tours of the college.

- Get information online about students' remarks and department profiles that pertain to *your* interest.

- Discuss *your* findings with your parents and the counselor.

Learning to Follow Through

This is an area that can be one of the most important skills for a student to learn. Many young students are procrastinators; therefore, they need instruction as to how to plan a follow through. The following are ways to develop promptness in planning:

- *A student* should keep a calendar of daily events and assignments. I suggest buying a large wall calendar and placing it on the wall in his/her room. You, the parent, can require that he/she mark this calendar daily with checks beside the activity or assignment as "finished" or "done" until it becomes routine for them. This requirement, at first, must have a consequence, if not done. Tell him/her what the consequence will be (not going out with their friends on the weekend), should they fail to do this task. This routine will become a daily visual cue, and be a constant reminder or scorecard for how he/she is doing with assignments.

- A student should make a log that lists activities, estimated duration time, and a start and finish date.

- A student needs instruction as to how to organize activities and responsibilities. At first they need supervision, encouragement and a complete explanation of accountability.

- A student should listen to these instructions and understand that this skill is not just a school thing, but a life thing. This skill learned early will only make his/her life easier.

- Parents should treat this learning the same as a chore. Consequences will follow if it is not followed through.

Learning to Meet Deadlines

- A student must keep a log of deadlines and note what to do before the deadline. This list should be visible, possibly a chart on the wall, to be a reminder of what comes next. A table calendar by month is a great way to see the weeks and flip to each month. Using the calendar on a cell phone may be a preferred system, but the student must make the effort to look at this calendar.

- Getting serious about being aware of time is the real key. The only way to do this is to get in the habit of checking your calendar daily, especially before going to bed. Make additions and changes daily.

- The punishment for not meeting deadlines is the obvious: A score of "O" on class work or points taken off.

- Be early and not late in meeting deadlines or risk not getting into that preferred college or getting that great job. There is no rule that you must wait until that exact deadline date to turn something in. Remember, "The early bird catches the worm"!

Learning to Work With Parents Towards a Common Goal

- Students should be made aware that the college application process is a family affair. Parents are still in charge, since they financially support their student. Students should be thankful that their parents are so supportive of this costly activity called "college."

- Students should share the goals and needs that they feel are a focus of their future college years. Parents should be supportive of this dialogue and be patient while discussing this with the student. Students should be somewhat "humble" since they are being given a gift (going to college).

- After meeting with the counselor, students should report the results. Parents should help with researching, but not actually do it. Parents should allow the student to gather the facts in order to be the biggest part of this process. This allows the student the experience of acquiring the knowledge necessary to make intelligent, informed decisions.

Learning to Coordinate Between Teachers, the Counselor, and Parents

- Students are caught in this triangle, whether they like it or not. So, it's important to make it a smooth ride by accepting the situation and taking advantage of parent, counselor, and teacher expertise, advice and support.

- Teachers can write great recommendations, but the student must show the teacher that he/she goes the extra mile in the classroom. Giving the teacher some nuts and bolts to write about will certainly give the student extra points in the application process.

- The Counselor needs to know the student. A student can get to know the counselor by dropping into the guidance office for scholarship forms and other information and spending some time sharing concerns or goals with him/her.

- Students can use their parents for support if they learn how to present their information in a positive light and consider suggestions made by their parents. Both parents and the student should be open during the research phase and allow themselves the luxury of discussion. Talk is cheap, but can give the student extra information to be used in making this important decision.

Learning Self Awareness

- Self-evaluation is one of the hardest things for a person to do. It takes a mature person to admit weaknesses and failures, and students in their youth guard against admissions. Strengths and weaknesses must be faced in order to write about oneself in an essay, improve on scoring and GPA, and improve on life skills that will yield success in the application process (learning to write, interview, make better grades, score better on standardized tests, organize, develop leadership abilities, meet deadlines, be accountable, work with professional and other adults).

- For a student to admit beyond the surface is a brave thing. The application process is a perfect place and time to do this. A good school or independent counselor can help the student gain confidence about overcoming weaknesses and improving their odds for the goal of college admission.

CHAPTER 7

I Want My Child to Go to Harvard!

Preplanning where a child will attend college takes a lot of work and there are no guarantees.

1. The child may or may not **cooperate academically**.

2. The cost for **tutors** and **preparation courses** may be beyond ones budget.

3. The school may or may not fit the student's **personality, academic skills and/or socialization**.

4. The student may or may not handle that **level of competition** well.

5. The **culture, religious and other belief systems** of **your** student may or may not parallel the school environment.

6. The **parent's social life** may or may not benefit from their student attending an Ivy League college.

7. **Private and elite preschools** may or may not be possible according to budget and/or location.

8. It may be *your* dream, but not your child's dream
    to go to Harvard.

Genes may give your child the ability to achieve a high GPA. Coupled with the correct learning environment and willingness by the child can result in academic success. If you have this perfect scenario, you might feel compelled to want your child to go to an Ivy League or equivalent school. There is more to this picture than the obvious:

- Your child makes *good grades and learning comes easy* and he/she may succeed well with assigned learning. But, it takes a special personality to possess the desire for learning and not just for a grade/reward. Maturity is another factor that parents should consider as well as competition with peers of equal ability.

- Decisions to use a *tutor* are made not only to help the student, but to indirectly help the teacher and eliminate parent stress. There are ways to cut costs in this process. A parent can hire a peer, or an upperclassman. A small fee could be paid to this student or any reward arrangements that you deem appropriate. For some families, expensive tutors, courses and learning centers are not an option. For those who do pay, there is no guarantee that your child will put forth the effort to take full advantage of time and money spent.

- College environments on Ivy League and competitive school campuses promote a *style of learning* for students who are there for the sake of learning, participating, and being academically active as opposed to learning for a grade or GPA to help get into graduate school. Your child may not fit this mode, no matter how academically smart they are.

- The social element is not only a consideration in college placement; it will encompass ninety percent of your student's life on campus. For this reason, the social aspect is very important to consider in choosing colleges to apply to.

- Your student might make good grades, but if he/she went to a *less competitive high school*, was supported heavily by *parents* to succeed, is not motivated, organized, has poor study habits, or does not learn beyond assignments, then you need to consider these important facts about your child suggesting a certain college environment. It is important to consider the ways in which your student learns, the academic tools they have developed, and how much of a challenge they are willing to handle.

- If your student is a *high achiever* that studies hard for grades, they may be in an awkward position for choosing a college. If you suggest and promote highly competitive colleges, you are asking your student to continue this academic struggle to achieve a high grade. The choice is simply this: If your student struggled and made good grades, you can help place them in a highly competitive college where they may struggle to make a B or C and not be at the top of the class (GPA may be lower for applying to graduate school). Or you can suggest a tier down in a college where they can still be challenged, but, they'll maintain the ability to achieve A's and remain at the top of the class. It's important to make sure your student has a positive college experience. This will eliminate undo stress in an undergraduate program.

CHAPTER 8

How to Plan for Admissions at Highly Competitive Colleges and Universities

- **Plan your curriculum** to include higher-level courses (use the advice of the counselor, teachers, and parents).

- If your high school does not offer a certain upper level course of a subject you like, look for an **online course or local college to dual enroll**.

- Get a **tutor** for your weak classes (student or hired professional tutor).

- Participate in **study groups** that include strong academic students.

- Keep a **calendar or spreadsheet** to track your academic schedule and deadlines **(teaches organization and reduces stress)**.

- *Preplan and organize* readings ahead of time (books, assignments and course chapters). Also, outline chapters and lectures (helps to remember what was read and is a good study sheet for exams).

- Determine what your *learning style* is and use it to gain academic success. Are you a visual, auditory (learn best by hearing information), or tactile (learn best through moving, doing, and touching) learner? Give yourself a reward (do something you enjoy) when you have completed your work. Decide if studying with one person or a group of people is your style. *Academic success is the goal, and reduction of stress.*

Imp

- Go beyond what is required. Read extra material for research papers, *bring articles* from newspapers and books for class discussion, etc. (Remember that *teachers write your recommendations* for college admissions and colleges like to hear that you go above and beyond requirements).

Imp

- Get to *know your guidance counselor*, for *she/he* is your advocate and the voice of your high school. *She/he* will rate how you stack up to your classmates academically. *Her/his recommendation* will also be filled with information about you personally and your role within the school.

- Set your *priorities*. Plan how you will handle the week. If you have activities after school, then your scheduled *study time* will be in the evenings. If there are days without after school activities, then treat the day as a *full workday*. When returning home from school, take a *break* for thirty minutes. Then, continue your homework until dinner time. Then the evening is yours. On days where the workload is too heavy and runs into the evening, always stop for *30 minutes before going to bed* and do something you enjoy before going to sleep. For some students, *waking at 5:30 a.m.* or so is a better time to finish work. *Find the schedule* each week that fits you. Also, treat Friday afternoon as a workday so that the rest of your weekend will be more leisurely.

Imp

Preparing For College Admissions

As you begin to fill out your college applications, a few guidelines may make the process a little easier. Little things are often overlooked, so these reminders may be helpful as you go along.

A. Read Directions

Pay attention to the specific directions for each application. Don't work on auto-pilot. A specific application can throw you a curve and too much white out doesn't look good. It is acceptable to use a paper copy or send the application electronically. Before sending the application, have it reviewed by a counselor and your parents.

B. Pay Attention to Deadlines

A college can decide not to accept a late application. Different parts of an application may have different deadlines, such as the supplements to the Common Application, Teacher Evaluation Forms, and Counselor Evaluation Forms. If you are interested in a Military Academy, the recommendation requirements will begin in the second semester of your junior year. If you plan to play sports, you must register with the NCAA Clearinghouse before you begin your college sport. The deadlines for standardized testing (SAT I, SAI II, ACT) should begin the second semester of your junior year. Keep a log of the deadlines of all college (private and public) scholarships. Also, Early Action, Early Decision and Regular Decision all have different deadlines according to the school. It is very important to cross reference the web, books and the college itself, if necessary to verify the correct dates.

C. Don't Procrastinate

Time is of the essence. Not only will procrastination build stress and create a situation in which your parents will constantly remind you to fill out applications, but if you procrastinate, you'll end up rushing to fulfill college deadlines at the same time as your senior year tests and deadlines.

D. Neatness is a Virtue

If you have to fill out a paper copy of an application, make it legible. Fill out a trial copy, if necessary, and then duplicate your responses on the final application to be submitted to eliminate having to make corrections. Remember that neatness can extend into the areas of grammar, spelling and punctuation. If you do not know what a word means, do not use it. The overall look of your application, including the essays and short answers are reflective on who you are and how you present yourself.

E. Keep All Correspondence

Keep and date all information that you and a prospective college have exchanged. If it has been by e-mail, print each individual message. Colleges receive an enormous number of applications. This can lead to a few mistakes. You want to be able to prove that you sent or received a document by a certain date.

F. Organization is the Key

Staying organized is the easiest way to stay on top of your applications. Keep each application in a separate folder and keep track on a calendar of all earlier deadlines- so you won't put things off.

G. E-Mail Address

Use your e-mail to communicate with colleges for information, especially with the admissions counselor or department head. If your questions or needed information are worth the college personnel time, then by all means show your interest in this way. Most students have an e-mail address. For those who do not, create one to receive information from the colleges. It is important to have an e-mail that is appropriate and without offensive language.

CHAPTER 9

Testing

Standardized testing consists of the **PSAT, PLAN, ACT, SAT I, SAT II, AP**. Preparation for these tests involves **time management** (working faster than normal and working under pressure.) Take practice tests with these things in mind so **your** time and test taking skills will improve.

PSAT

Colleges never see these scores. **The student** should take the PSAT in the sophomore year for practice and the junior year to compete for the **National Merit Scholarship**. There are practice tests online at **www.collegeboard.com**.

PLAN

The PLAN test is administered in the fall of the sophomore year. It is a predictor of success on the ACT. At the same time, it focuses on career preparation and academic achievement. This achievement test has four sections: English, Mathematics, Reading and Science. More information is found online at **www.act.org**.

ACT

This is a **curriculum-based** test for college admissions that has four sections: **English, Math, Reading, and Science Reasoning** (highest total composite is 36). There is an **optional writing portion** and a **career inventory** (only filled out once). There is an **ACT Online Prep** which has practice tests with real ACT test questions—find the practice tests at **www.act. org**. ACT allows the student to send in scores for up to **four colleges free**. The student must pay extra for additional schools. **In most colleges, the ACT is not super scored.**

SAT I

This is a **reasoning test** used for college admissions. It consists of three sections: **Critical Reading, Math and Writing** (800 point maximum in each section with total composite equaling to 2400). Practice tests are found online at **www.collegeboard.com**. A student should take the SAT I **(two to three times in the spring and summer of the junior year and fall of the senior year)**. If the SAT I is taken before the spring of the junior year, it is fine for practice. If there is more than one set of scores sent to a college, they will **super score** the test (take the highest score from each section from more than one test and recalculate a composite score). This is the advantage of taking the test more than once. The College Board allows up to **four colleges** to receive your scores **free**. **Each time you take the test, you must list these schools again and any additional schools to receive the most recent scores.**

SAT II

Finally a test you can really study for. These subject tests **(English Mathematics, History, Science, and Foreign Language, etc.)** demonstrate to the colleges the student's mastery of content and provide a dependable measure of the student's academic achievement. For this reason, a ninth grade student should begin to think about scheduling and taking the SAT II. Though the requirements for each college is different, it is good to **take four to six of these tests** in subjects you are strong in, so that **your** best scores are used by the colleges during admissions. These tests are **one hour long per subject** and a student can take up to three in one morning. I would suggest that students only take two in one morning, **so they can do their best** and not become tired in the last hour. Purchase SAT II **preparation books** for each subject to have a study guide **(knowledge is the key)**.

SAT II's are used by the college in conjunction to what teachers say in a recommendation. This test also sorts out a standard across the nation. This test will either backup what is presented in the student's file or contradict it. If you are an **underachiever**, using these results, colleges will perceive you as smart and may take a chance on you in hopes you would blossom in college.

AP

Students taking an AP course in high school show the college that they have **challenged themselves** academically. In addition, if students do well on the AP exam at the end of the course, they will demonstrate a level of **academic mastery** in that course, which will grant **college academic credit (possible to enter with sophomore status in a student's first year)**. Colleges vary in acceptance numbers for credit (3 to 5). The number of AP courses to be taken is based on the number of AP classes that are available to the student, either through choice or schedule conflicts. If students cannot schedule a specific AP class, then they can buy a **practice book** for each course and study to prepare for the AP test, even though they did not take the course. Circumstances should always be presented by the **counselor in her recommendation letter to explain the reason why the student was unable to take the course** (prior commitment of time, scheduling problems, did not care for the teacher teaching the AP, wanted to budget time in other subjects to secure or raise GPA, etc.) A student should *choose an AP course from each academic group* and then take other AP classes according to interest. Colleges look at academic challenging that incorporates taking AP's in many subjects. However, if you are weak in an area of study, it is better to earn a high grade in a regular or honors class then make a poor grade in an AP. AP semester grades are inflated by many high schools. Most colleges ask for a weighted and an un-weighted GPA. All in all, the actual grade is recorded on the transcript, regardless of the weight. Colleges see students that choose to take many AP classes as students who challenge themselves and are *eager to learn beyond the required courses in a high school*.

CHAPTER 10

Special Talents

How will a special talent help you in admissions? It is important to send your tape or other materials to the specific college department and inform them that you are applying for admission and would appreciate a letter of support to admissions if the department feels that your work warrants that recommendation. I cannot emphasize strongly enough that your talent needs to be superior and not just that you learned an instrument or danced or have taken art for a few years. Know yourself and your level of ability. One way you can do this is to consult with your teachers and instructors in the field. Also, attend special summer programs to learn your art better and to compare your work to others who are in your age range. It just makes you aware of your status at the time and whether you have peaked or can advance.

If you choose to use a talent to help in the admissions process and scholarships, you should extend beyond your normal routine, which will result in refining your talent and also relay to the admissions committee that you went outside the box. The decision to send extra examples of your talent can be determined by two things. First, are you planning to use your talent on campus? Second, are you extremely talented in this area? If the answer to both of these questions is "yes," then you should send in any additional materials. Ask your teacher/instructors how you compare to other students your age—ask for an "honest assessment".

How does a talent factor into the decision process for admissions? It shows your passion and offers diversity and involvement on campus. These two things are valued by competitive colleges. This, of course is only a piece of the formula, but an important one that can separate you from other students.

CHAPTER 11

The Activity List
(better known as the resumé)

An impressive *resumé* shows commitment to activities through longevity ("longevity" refers to how many years you have invested in a particular talent or skill). Observe examples of top students' pursuits and think about competing on the state and/or national level in recognition. Refer to *leadership*, be a founder of a new activity, spur others into action, go beyond your boundaries within your interests (do extra research, readings, shadow a professional, get a job concentrated in this area of interest, start your own business—even a lawn business—raise money for a good cause that is tied into your interest, etc.).

This list should show your true passions and talents. Remember to concentrate on depth and breadth, not quantity of activities. Colleges look for *students who will become involved in campus life and will influence and lead their peers*. This should be foremost in your mind when participating in an activity, sport, art, community work or any such interests. It is important to not only engage in your chosen activities, but it's more important to transfer your experience into a leadership role by creating a project that is original or unique. A student who has gone beyond to become involved, create or develop will gain points in the admissions process. *The great advantage of doing this is your own self-development and learned life skills. This is your chance to tell an admissions officer about your:*

- *passions outside of school*

- *your degree of intellectual curiosity*

- *your leadership ability*

- *your initiative*

- *your expertise*

- *your time commitment*

- *your love of learning*

- *your ability to be a mover and shaker*

Admissions officers look at your activity list to get a sense of who you are in terms of your character and personality. If you choose an activity or interest that is different from the mainstream, explain about it in detail. Competitive colleges like unusual interests and hobbies. They do report statistical information among their competitors that include unusual and unique activities and interests by the incoming freshman class. These interests can range from a fire thrower to an Internet CEO of a start up e-mail business. *I cannot emphasize enough how important it is for you to take your interest or hobby to the next level of development! Colleges do not want a well-rounded student, they want a well-rounded class. So, be the top singer or instrument player in your school, etc.*

How to Set Up the Activity List

- At the head of a document, include your name, SSN, date of birth, high school name, e-mail address and phone number.

- Organize your activities on a scrap sheet of paper and list and categorize them, (the head may say music and then you block off sections underneath the heading to list and describe all of your involvement in music). The blocked off sections are labeled as follows:

Activity | School Years | Hours per-week/ | Position | Description
                              Hours per-year

- The Description column should be bigger than the rest of the columns. Use a ten-point font to allow your description to fit in the space.

- Colleges will sometimes request on their application for you to list the activities in order of importance to you.

- When writing the descriptions, your first few sentences should explain the activity followed by what you did and accomplished within that activity. Make sure you use a natural conversational tone that is not formal. Remember, they want to understand your character and personality. But make sure to use correct grammar and spell words correctly.

- Do not exaggerate. ***These activities and interests should be specifically mentioned and elaborated on by teachers and counselors in their recommendations. If this is not the case, you may come across as exaggerating, which will not be favorable on your behalf!***

- In the description, do not make statements like, "It was meaningful to me."

- Use active verbs like, "I collated," "I led." "I rounded up," "I created," etc.

- If you were part of a team word it like this, "I was one of three students who…"

- For competitive sports state the accomplishment, "Our team finished first."

- If you started a company or business, state that. This shows great initiative.

- Use spell check.

- Avoid clichés.

ACTIVITY LIST (RESUMÉ)

Name
Address
City, State, Zip Code
Home Phone Number
Cell Number
E-Mail Address

I.	**Education**	**School Years**	**Positions/Honors**
	Name of High School	9, 10, 11, 12	

II.	**Extra Curricular**	**School Years**	**Positions/Honors**
	Volleyball	9, 10, 11, 12	
	Basketball	9, 10, 11, 12	
	Key Club	12	President
	Junior Club	11	Class Representative
	Spanish Club	11	Treasurer
	SGA	11, 12	Vice-President
	National Honor Society	10, 11, 12	

III.	**Awards/Honors**	**School Years**	**Honors/Title**
	National Honor Roll	9, 10, 11, 12	
	Girls State Nominee	11	
	Academic Award	11	
	Art Award	10, 11	
	Varsity Volleyball	11, 12	Captain(11)

IV.	**Community Service**	**School Years**	**Hrs. Per Week/Per Year**	**Positions**
	Sunday School Teacher	10, 11, 12	2/80	Teacher of 5 year olds
	Nursing Home	10		Played Piano
	Y.M.C.A. Volunteer	11		After School Program

V.	**Summer Experience**	**School Years**	**Hrs. Per Week/Per Year**	**Description**
	Basketball Camps	10,11	5/100	Improve game

VI.	**Hobbies/Interests**	**School Years**	**Hrs. Per Week/Per Year**	
	Tennis	9, 10, 11, 12	2/100	
	Knitting	10, 11, 12		
	Painting	9, 10, 11, 12		

VII.	**Employment**	**School Year**	**Hrs. Per Week/Per Year**	**Positions**
	Animal Clinic	10, 11	6/280	Assisted the Vets

VIII.	**Travel**	**School Years**	**Description**
	Washington D.C.	11	Smithsonian Summer Program

CHAPTER 12

The Essay

You are the primary focus of the essay. This is your chance to shine. Write something that the reader can learn from. Remember, the admissions officers have so many essays to read and may get bored during this tedious process. You must show your passion and relate it to their college or your future. Keep the short answer essay brief and to the point. If you mention anything specific about their college, be sure it is specific and that you have researched it online to gather accurate facts. Avoid using clichés and give details instead. The following is a sample from a college essay:

"From a very young age, I was always interested in learning about what caused some phenomena. As I grew, I learned about a word called 'research' which meant that it was an organized way to find out and experiment to learn. In middle school, I remember chills going up and down my spine in excitement as I entered my first lab class. As I began to learn more about the sciences, I discovered that Biological Science was interesting to me because it's not only relative to us, but its findings give us hope for our future in helping to provide a better quality of life and possible longevity. For this reason, research fascinated me and I began shadowing a physician doing research on Type II Diabetes. I learned that Stem Cell research, where physicians can take a patients own skin cells and inject them into the diabetic patient, can help reverse the diabetes. During my junior year, I took Mr. Smith's AP Biology class. His enthusiasm and expertise stimulated my interest to learn more in the biological sciences. It is this caliber of class that I look forward to at your college."

If you choose to write about the person who most influenced you or a traumatic experience that changed you, you **MUST TALK ABOUT YOURSELF**. The admissions officers are not interested in the event itself or the other person. The reason the essay portion was created was to give you an opportunity to write about yourself and to allow the admissions officers to understand who you are in terms of character. Make sure you write in the first person and the essay focuses on you. Your choice can be an event that happens to you daily, but always has an impact on you. Try to showcase your intellectual curiosity. Express yourself with confidence. This is your chance to stand out from other students; it is not an English essay for the teacher to compare your work with other students. The admission officers are looking for what distinguishes you from the other essays they are reading. Remember, they read hundreds of essays and just like you, do not want to be bored. In your essay, implement the next three categories:

The 8 B's

1. Be thoughtful.

2. Be personal.

3. Be insightful (more insights, less generalizations).

4. Be revealing.

5. Be yourself.

6. Be adolescent.

7. Be journalistic; crisp, clear, clean.

8. Be psychological.

The 8 Thinks

1. Think micro, not macro (more insights, less descriptions).

2. Think about what you think about yourself.

3. Think about what you think about others.

4. Think: How have I grown? Not, what have I done?

5. Think about your opinions.

6. Think "me", not "we".

7. Think about your values.

8. Think more about your learning and less time about the topic to choose.

The 6 Actions

1. Demonstrate your philosophies.

2. Show vulnerability.

3. Write and let it flow. Do not try to be perfect.

4. Tell what you have learned.

5. A significant event may last only five minutes or it may have lasted your entire life.

6. If choosing between traditional and risky, choose risky.

10 Additional Things to Remember When Writing Your Essay

1. **Look at your application as a whole**—Don't repeat your activity list or resumé in your short or long essays. The person

reading your application should see the real you without repetitive lists. Likewise, do not write about your passion for a certain career if you have not taken the appropriate courses to prepare you for that major—there should be concordance between your past and your goals for the future.

2. **Decide what makes you different**—the more competitive the admissions process, the more important your uniqueness will be. The college will be looking at what you contribute to the community. The more specific you are about your feelings, experiences and dreams, the more unique you will sound. For example, if you want to go into business, you will sound like everyone else. If you tell them that you want to open a restaurant, you will stand out. If you tell them that you want to study business so you can open a Cajun restaurant with recipes handed down from your grandmother, they'll be more interested in letting you in, so they can be a part of this very meaningful venture and possibly enjoy its benefits. Your goals will seem specific, but be genuine.

3. **Write about what you know**—your essays will be stronger and more impressive if your focus on subjects you know well. Don't try to guess what the admission officer wants to read. An admission officer reading thousands of essays a year can detect an essay that sounds too embellished and not realistic. Also, if your grades, scores, and recommendations are not consistent with your writing style, there may be some suspicion that you did not write the essay. Because details and examples make a strong essay, writing about a topic you do not know much about will result in a generic essay that anyone could have written. Write about a person or place that you know well so that your description can include all five senses and details that will make your essay come alive.

4. **Write about what you care about**—Your passion and commitment to one or two areas of your life will be the most important aspects of your essay. Show the reader who you really are and what you value. Remember, if you have to do research to write about a topic, choose another topic. If you are asked to write about a world problem, write about the homeless man you see everyday rather than cigar-rollers in Nicaragua—unless you have been a cigar-roller.

5. **Show**, **don't tell**—You have only a few minutes to capture the interest and attention of the admission reader. Don't waste those minutes with a boring essay telling them how wonderful you are! Show them—write from the heart. Rather than tell the reader that a person you know is stubborn, tell them a story that illustrates the person's stubbornness. Stories are memorable and are the best way to show your personality as well as the personality of the person you are describing. Admission committees admit specific people rather than someone who can check all the boxes on the application. Stories make you a real person.

6. **Personalize all essays**—The admission reader is not interested in reading about something taking place outside of your life, but rather wants to know about the events in your life. If your grades were terrible in the ninth grade, explain how and why you matured from the experience. If you have had a wonderful or terrible thing happen to you, write about it in the light of what you learned from it. Do not be afraid to tell everything. Just be sure to put it in the perspective of how you will apply this new knowledge to your future behavior.

7. **Have fun, be creative, be interesting**—Think about your reader and the huge stack of other essays waiting to be read. If you want to capture your audience, you need to keep it in mind when you write. Think about adding a little boost to that

person's otherwise boring day. Do not lose track of number four. Maybe an essay is not the best format to say what you want to say. Are you a good poet? Write a poem. You should use your best talent in presenting yourself.

8. **Rewrite, then rewrite again**—You may be in the habit of writing school papers at the last minute, but your application will be judged on your readiness to do well in university level academic work. A sloppy essay thrown together in haste will not be judged worthy of acceptance to a competitive university. Start working on essays as soon as the common application or specific school application is ready online. Usually the middle of July to the middle of September is when the new applications become available. Summer has some great moments to use your time to think about yourself and who you are. That way, you can approach any essay question with yourself in mind.

9. **Ask a few people for their comments**—Ask your parents, friends, English teacher, and counselor to read your final attempt. Do not bore them with a dozen drafts.

10. **Ask yourself if something is missing**—Re-read the whole application and look for unanswered questions. Is there anything about yourself that you feel would be valuable for the college counselor to know? Did the application ask you all the questions that you wanted to answer? Before finishing all the work on your application, make sure that you have said all the things that the reader needs to know about you.

Things to Consider:

• Because you've done something wonderful does not mean you will (or should) write an essay about it.

- Ask yourself, "What would everyone else say if they were writing about your topic?" Then immediately discard all of that and write your story about the topic.

- Take a position and say what you think.

> **Most important:** *You can never write too many drafts for your college essay.*

CHAPTER 13

Helpful Hints For Letters of Recommendations

- In deciding who to ask to write your recommendations, choose a teacher who is from your junior or senior year.

- It is better if you get a recommendation from a teacher that has been involved with you outside the classroom, such as having worked on a special project. *v. Imp*

- Many teachers like to work on the recommendations over the summer, so begin asking in the spring of your junior year.

- If you apply early decision or early action, you will need to ask at the beginning of your senior year if you did not ask in your junior year.

- Remind your recommendation -writing teachers that colleges are looking for your participation in the classroom and want specific examples of your achievement rather than vague praise.

- Give counselors a resumé of your activities and accomplishments to help them with an overview of your high school accomplishments and contributions. If your grades fell during a certain period of time, you should explain this to the counselor and tell him/her how you have changed or improved.

In preparation for the recommendation part of your application:

 - Approach teachers and the counselor at least **_three weeks prior_** to needing to send the recommendation.

- Provide each teacher, the counselor and any additional persons with the following information:

  a. A copy of your resumé.

  b. Teacher Evaluation Sheet (provided by the college online or attached to the paper copy of the application).

  c. Counselor Evaluation Sheet (provided by the college online or attached to the paper copy of the application).

  d. A handwritten thank-you note that includes your contact information, the date the recommendation should be sent to each college, to whom the letter is to be addressed, if so instructed, and instructions of whether to send the recommendations directly to the college or give it to the counselor to send. Since recommendations are confidential, it is not procedure for the recommendations to be given to you to mail.

- Include the following requests to those writing the recommendations:

  a. Print on school letterhead.

  b. Sign each copy of the letter.

  c. Save the letter in the event additional copies may be requested.

- Include an addressed and stamped envelope to be given to your teachers writing the recommendations for each college if you need for them to send it directly to the colleges.

- In the event you decide to complete scholarship applications, you will need to mention to your teachers and your counselor that you may ask them to modify their letter of recommendation for the scholarship recommendation. Follow the procedure above for providing the proper timeline and materials.

- Provide teachers and counselors with deadlines for each recommendation that you are requesting, especially noting the earliest deadline.

- Typically, you know your teachers well enough to determine who can provide a favorable review of your accomplishments. If in doubt, don't hesitate to ask if they feel comfortable writing a recommendation. In some cases, you may have no choice as to who to use, but when you do, make the best choice possible. If you are in real question, ask other students advice, especially recently graduated students.

- Follow up with your recommendation writers a week or so prior to your first deadline, to ensure recommendations have been mailed or to see if they need additional information from you.

- On your application form, there is usually a space for you to mark if you want to see the recommendation that your teacher or counselor has written. I feel that you should answer "no", *Imp* that you do not wish to see the essay. This relays to the college that you trust the person that you asked to write a recommendation. Additionally, this gives more credibility to the recommendation in the eyes of the college.

- Once you have decided which college to attend, hand write thank-you notes to everyone who provided a recommendation and tell them where you have decided to go to college. Do not send e-mail thank you notes. Be sure and do this before graduation day.

CHAPTER 14

If I am a Privileged Kid!

When applying to highly selective schools, it is important to know that the admission officers read applications from students that have had many advantages of private schools, expensive summer programs, boarding schools, expensive summer camps, and students who have traveled to various places in the world. The people reading your application may not have had these opportunities. If your application, essay and resumé primarily reflect those privileges, then it will only show that your parents provided you with these opportunities. It is important that your ability and efforts demonstrate your growth and accomplishments. You want to avoid any prejudice against you because of your status or privilege. There are ways to do this:

For example, get a job—Something that ties in with your interests such as working in a music store if music is your thing. Try to start working at the beginning of high school to prevent the appearance of only doing this for admissions purposes. Avoid more glamorous jobs. Start your own business (yard work or computer). Try to work during each summer. If you choose to shadow someone to learn a business and then take those skills and start your own business, it will show that you reached a high level of competency and will show that you not only have a passion for that area of interest, but are taking the initiative and have the drive to go beyond just learning. It is important to show a love of learning. ***Implementation is the key!***

Remember, the admissions officers are there to learn about your character as well as your abilities. It is up to you to show yourself to be a hard working and committed person who has made a difference and matured because of it.

CHAPTER 15

Funding College!

College and Career Nights are attended by many junior and senior high school students each year. As these students and parents visit each college desk, they are enthralled by the literature and filled in about all the wonderful opportunities that particular college has in store for any student that **wants** to attend. Requirements for applying (GPA and standardized scores are mentioned), but the promotion of the school is the real pitch.

Colleges and universities are businesses and just like all other businesses, it is important to market your product in hopes to attract the right kind of customers. Unlike someone selling a product with a fixed price, colleges and universities can't know how much it may cost you because there are so many variables that impact "total cost." Some colleges sound so expensive that they seem untouchable to some students and families. Others seem reasonable, but extra aid may not be in the picture. If you qualify, the largest amount of money to be awarded will come from the university or college merit scholarships. To have other scholarship opportunities, you can choose to explore the various scholarships and contests available.

There are two sites that list many scholarship opportunities: *Fast Web (www.fastweb.com)*, and *College Board (www.collegeboard.com)*

The Fast Web, a safe and trusted site, provides a free search for scholarships, tools and tips to help pay for college and help in finding jobs and internships for students. College Board, known for being the administrators of the SAT I, provides a free scholarship search. Both sites are easy to use.

Many of these scholarships yield relatively small amounts of money. One must take the time to research and fill out the scholarship forms with essays, which may be required. There is no guarantee of winning.

If a scholarship requires money to apply, then it is a SCAM. If a scholarship asks for your personal financial information, you should avoid that scholarship. In addition to your own search for scholarships, there are many opportunities sent to the high school counselor's office. Students and parents should inquire about these scholarships beginning in the tenth grade. There are some counselors that include scholarship opportunities on the high school monthly web site. If you are interested in a particular college, notify your high school counselor of your interest in being nominated for that college scholarship.

The following is a partial list of scholarships from the website, www.scholarships4students.com. These scholarships can be searched and filled out through out the high school years, in hopes of earning money for college. It does take a great deal of effort, so look at this as a job that will earn you money. This is a website that I am not promoting but is an example of a list of scholarships that you can choose to research.

Scholarships for High School Students
(These are subject to change)

- College Prowler Monthly Scholarship

- Coca Cola's $25,000 College Bound Scholarship

- A GPA Isn't Everything Scholarship

- College Prowler "No Essay" Scholarship

- Frame My Future Scholarship

- Ashley Marie Easterbrook Scholarship

- NF1B Young Entrepreneur Award

- Herman and Katherine Peters Foundation Scholarship

- Discover Scholarship Program

- Brickfish "Off Road Nation" Contest

- Best Buy Scholarship

- Opray's National High School Essay Contest

- The Fountainhead Essay Contest

- Signet Classics Scholarship Essay Contest

- Traditional Family Coalition Essay Contest

- The Christopher's "You Can Make A Difference" Poster Contest

- American Legion National High School Oratorical Contest

- America's Junior Miss Scholarship Program

- McKelvey Entrepreneurial Foundation — e- Scholarship

- Brickfish "Be a Milk Rock Star with Rascal Flatts!" Scholarship

- Toyota Community Scholars Program

- Brickfish "Give Your Party Some Props!" Scholarship

- Excellence Through Ethics Essay Contest

- Brickfish "I Can't Live Without My..." Scholarship

- AXA Acheivement Community Scholarship

- Brickfish "I Deserve $1000 Because" Scholarship

- U.S. Bank Internet Scholarship Program

- Brickfish Family and Friends Photo Campaign Scholarship

- Walt Disney Company Foundation Scholarship

- The National WWII Museum On-Line Student Essay Contest

- CBAI Annual Scholarship Program

- Sterling Honorary Award

- Making It Count "Winning Characteristics" Scholarship

- Kohl's Kids Who Care Award

- Bruce Lee Award

- Help Santa Find the Real Tree Contest

- NetAid Global Action Awards

- Brickfish "Design a T-Shirt for Honest Foods!" Scholarship

- American Heroes—U.S. Military Challenge

- Youth Foundation Scholarship

- Brickfish Ultimate Fashion Challenge

- Brickfish If You Only Heard It Coming Contest

- National Vocabulary Championship

- Red Vines Drawing Contest

- Junior Achievement Nelnet Scholarship

- Maryknoll Student Essay Contest

- Gloria Barron Prize for Young Heroes

- KFC Colonel's Scholars Scholarship

- Courageous Persuaders Scholarship

- Apple Scholars Program

- Duck Brand Duct Tape Stuck at Prom Contest

- High School Graduation Speech Contest

- Siemens Westinghouse Competition

- Lemonade Series Writing Scholarship

- Anthem Essay Contest

- "What is Your Dream for the World in 2020" Contest

- National High School Poetry Contest

- "My Turn" Essay Contest

- Imation Computer Arts Scholarship

- Students Helping Students "I Can Make a Difference" Scholarship

- Junior Achievement "Excellence Through Ethics" Essay Contest

- Robert C. Byrd Honors Scholarship

- Holocaust Remembrance Project Essay Contest

- Fountainhead Essay Contest

- Hugh B. Sweeney Scholarship

- Junior Achievement "Excellence Through Ethics" Essay Contest

- Young Naturalist Award

- Guidepost Young Writers Contest

- NSSAR Knight Essay Contest

- The 7th Generation Community Service Scholarship Program

- Voice of Democracy Audio Essay Contest

- John F. Kennedy Profile in Courage Essay Contest

- AAA Travel High School Challenge

- Eco-Hero Award

- AFSA National Scholarship Essay Contest

- DuPont Challenge Science Essay Competition

- Stuck at Prom Contest

- George S. & Stella M. Knight Essay Contest

- First Freedom Student Scholarship

- Angel Soft Angels in Action Award

- Atlas Shrugged Essay Contest

- Free Speech and Democracy Film Contest

- National Peace Essay Contest

- Federal Junior Duck Stamp Art Competition

- Sam Walton Community Scholarship

- Americanism Essay Contest

- Alert Magazine Drug/Alcohol Abuse Prevention Essay Contest

- Rice Romp Essay Contest

- America Loves Math Scholarship Contest

- ExploraVision Science Competition

- Optimist International Essay Contest

- Young Epidemiology Scholars Competition

- Most Valuable Student Competition

The Scholarship Game

1. Those who fund scholarships do not always run their own scholarship program. The administrators may be another group and the judges may be still another group.

2. Gain knowledge of the various types of scholarships and the ones that fit you. They can vary and include sports, the arts, oratory, debate, government service, inventions, science projects, science research, history appreciation, creative writing, dance, graphic design, community service, computer programming, etc.

3. Research the numerous private sources of scholarships. Some can include, The American Legion, religious groups, Jaycees, Rotary Club, The Optimist Club, Garden Clubs, National Honor Society, Boy Scouts/Girl Scouts of America, military, Chamber of Commerce, Future Farmers of America, newspapers, banks, disability associations, business professionals, corporations, others based on geographic region, etc.

4. For some of the aforementioned, you must be a member or have some affiliation.

5. Some scholarships target students with specific future goals. If you are even marginally interested in a field, you should not hesitate to apply.

6. There are various scholarships for minorities, ethnic groups, sexes (mainly women or they may want one female and one male) and religions.

7. There are scholarships for disabilities.

8. There are scholarships for student employment, even part-time.

9. There are scholarships for winning contests like "Homecoming Queen".

10. There are scholarships for various "sports".

CHAPTER 16

Financial Aid Myths

The following will help your understanding of college cash flow which includes Financial Aid, scholarships, grants, and loans. It is important to dismiss any myths that exist so you can concentrate on the facts.

1. Myth: "Only low-income families get help for college expenses."

College financial aid administrators often take into account not only income, but also other family members in college, family size, assets, or unusual expenses.

Two types of aid:

    a. Need Based Aid—This type of aid considers need, but can be for low-income, middle-income, and high-income families. It focuses on "demonstrated need". That is, the more expensive a college, university, or technical school is, the more need-based aid you are eligible to receive.

b. Merit-Based Aid—This type of aid does not consider financial need. Interests, talents, achievements, personal qualities, activities, skills, and leadership are what are considered. What constitutes merit depends on who is awarding the money. Aid can be provided by colleges and the government, corporations, non-profit organizations, foundations, services clubs, and associations. *Merit takes GPA and scores into account*, but since there is no set formula, it can weigh the considerations listed above.

Conclusion: Never rule out a college or university because of its price tag! Also, many colleges will weigh both types of criteria—need plus merit.

2. Myth: "Only students with high GPA's can win merit based scholarships."

Many programs are *"grade blind."* Monies are awarded for various *talents, interests and efforts*, diverse endeavors in music, performing arts, foreign language, leadership, community service, photography, amateur radio, writing, science projects, oratory, debate, and part-time jobs. The scholarship may specify a certain GPA to qualify, like a 2.5, but once you qualify for that, you are able to compete. Programs consider a student's interest and study outside the traditional curriculum.

3. Myth: "Most scholarships are for athletes and minority students."

Scholarships geared toward athletes and minorities are only one small portion of the scholarship picture. Many scholarship providers will try to seek out students who have similar profiles to themselves.

4. Myth: "Once you've graduated from high school, it's too late."

During the four years of college, there are *general scholarships* for all students as well as those focused on *areas of interests* and *area of study*. This is true for graduate school as well. There are also scholarships for untraditional students going to school.

5. Myth: "Applying for scholarships is just like applying for college."

They both have similar components, but applying for a scholarship requires more *strategic planning*. When applying for scholarships, define what each program considers to be an "ideal applicant." You must implement tailor-made strategies that emphasize *personal attributes consistent with the scholarships goals*.

6. Myth: "Past actions and choices predetermine scholarship success."

What you do after you decide to apply for a scholarship is just as important as the record you have already accumulated. Your die has not been cast. Academically, you can *choose more strenuous courses in your junior and senior years*. In an *essay*, you can address why your academics were weak and how this created a character-building experience. Also, for *extracurricular activities*, you can concentrate in one area and create an example in which you took your talents and interests and formed an opportunity for *leadership and creativity*. An example as stated before, is when I had a student who was very proficient in Math. Taking just that element, he was able to create and teach math to high school teenager mothers who dropped out of school. This allowed them the opportunity to get their GED—and it helped him get a free ride at UVA and UNC at Chapel Hill.

7. Myth: "Focusing on a few awards maximizes your odds of winning."

Actually, it's a numbers game. You can leverage your time by *using previous essays as a reference for new essays, reusing lists you made, using the same recommendation* letters or forms you create. Once you have applied to a couple of scholarships, 60 % of the work to apply to ten is done. It is a *cumulative process*.

8. Myth: "You should not consider your first choice college if it costs too much."

Generally the higher the total college costs, the easier it is to demonstrate eligibility for financial aid. Private colleges often offer more financial aid to attract students from every income level.

9. Myth: "My parents will have to sell their house to pay for college."

Home value is not considered in calculations for federal financial aid. Colleges may take home equity into account when determining how much you are expected to contribute to college costs, but *income is a far greater factor*.

10. Myth: "Student's income will not affect financial aid."

Assets and income are defined the same for both students and parents. But, the student's wealth and cash flow are counted much more heavily...47% of parent's income and 5.6% of their assets, compared to 50% of the student's income and 35% of their assets. Debts are not deducted from assets to arrive at availability, unless they are secured by the asset.

According to the College Board, in the past ten years, tuition has gone up 51% at public universities and 34% at private schools, even after adjusting to inflation. In the past two decades, tuition has increased 115% at public and private schools alike.

CHAPTER 17

Understanding the Scholarship Jargon

1. **Loan**—Money you have to pay back.

2. **Subsidized Loan**—Awarded to those students with financial need. The borrower pays only a portion of the total interest payment or is exempt from the interest payment for a period of time. The government picks up the rest of the interest tab.

3. **Direct Stafford Loan**—A subsidized loan in which the Government pays the interest on your loan while you are in college and for the first six months after you leave school. You must qualify for payment deferments.

4. **Unsubsidized Loans**—Available to any family or student regardless of financial need, but you have to pay the full interest payment on your own with interest charged from the moment you assume the loan.

5. **Scholarships and Grants**—Allow students to choose their educational destiny regardless of their families financial

limitations. Scholarships and Grants do not have to be paid back. They are granted from Financial Aid private sources and are paid either to the student's institution of Higher Ed or directly to the student. Some are paid as a lump sum and some over four years in equal distribution. Scholarships and Grants given by the colleges, "Institutional Awards", are discounted off the schools sticker price. There are two categories of grants:

   a. **Pell Grant**—This is the largest need-based (demonstrated) grant sponsored by the U.S. Government. This awards money to lower-income families.

   b. Need-based scholarships and Grants issued by Colleges, State Governments, and Private Organizations.

6. Need Gapping—When colleges award a student only part of the financial aid needed in order to spread out aid money among more students.

How to Demonstrate Need

Ask one question: How does *your* family's financial resources compare to the cost of attending your desired school?

FAFSA

First, starting January 1 of *the student's* senior year in high school, fill out the *FAFSA* (Free Application for Federal Student Aid). This form can be found in the counselor's office at school or more conveniently, online at *www.fafsa.ed.gov.*

FAFSA aid is calculated based on a percentage of parents' income/assets, which is then divided by the number of members currently attending college. Then the government adds a percent of *the student's* own income and assets. *You* will then receive an assessment, the *SAR* (Student Aid Report) showing how much you are expected to contribute to the college **EFC** (Estimated Family Contribution). If the cost of the college **COA** (Cost of Attendance), is greater than what you are expected to contribute, then you have *"demonstrated"* financial need.

FAFSA Facts:

a. Fill out the form carefully (preferably to be sent after January 1 of the student's senior year) using last years return.

b. ***Sign it.***

c. Colleges have strict financial aid budgets which limit the amount of need- based scholarships and grants, so file the FAFSA as close to January 1 as possible.

d. The financial aid offices estimate "demonstrated need" very differently from the reality of the family cash flow and bank accounts.

e. Even though colleges advertise that they meet 100 % of need or print that a high percent of the student body receives financial aid, there is not much leverage on the student's part, which must depend on the income of the family and discretion of the financial aid office. Much of this aid is in the form of loans that must be paid back.

f. Since aid is distributed on a year-to-year basis, a student may receive a sizable financial aid package for the freshman year and then be offered a reduced aid package in subsequent years, when the student is less likely to transfer.

g. A web site that you can use, ***www.finaid.com***, will provide additional information and allow you to get a calculation of your EFC. Be sure to provide only the information they request as defined by the instructions.

h.   The reason to file the FAFSA is two fold:

   i. Without this data, many colleges cannot offer merit aid to the student.

   ii. If you have any change in finances during the year, without these numbers the college/university cannot help you.

Therefore, the more expensive the college, the greater amount of financial aid you are likely to receive.

CSS Profile (College Scholarship Service Profile)

www.profileonline.collegeboard.com: This is a college specific service used by private colleges and universities, graduate and professional schools and scholarship programs to award grant and scholarship money. The form is also found in the high school counselor's office or online at *www.collegeboard.com*. Click on *CSS/Profile*, then click the *year* that the student intends to enter as a freshman, then click on *Register for Profile*. Remain online and click on *Participating Institutions* to learn about the participating institutions and their priority filing date. Register at least two weeks prior to the college's earliest priority filing date. October 1 is the beginning filing date and all personal information received is only sent to the colleges or programs you authorize. According to College Board, your information is stored in a secure environment with firewall protection and is not shared with anyone. Unlike the FAFSA which is free, the CSS/Profile will cost $25.00 for the initial application and $16.00 for each additional college and/or program you designate. Cost is subject to change in the future. This college-specific financial aid application is similar to the FAFSA, but uses slightly different financial indicators.

Student Savings: Any savings account in the student's name is likely to affect the Estimated Family Contribution (EFC) since it is generally accepted that 50% of this goes to college expenses each year. Parental savings are reviewed at a much lower rate.

Preferential Packaging

Merit-based factors very often infiltrate the need-based application process. Therefore, since schools can set their own rules on aid, a student who can demonstrate more merit is much more likely to get the better financial aid package. This is also called, *"merit within need."*

Colleges do preferential packaging because it creates a domino affect:

1. The college/university feels this will encourage strong applicants to apply.

2. The school will then draw better faculty.

3. The school will then be able to have more research.

4. The school will then develop a better reputation.

5. The school will then be more competitive.

6. Strong students will become more supportive alumni.

7. Final result—School has a great endowment.

Why is gaining merit scholarships outside of the college so important?

Colleges don't consider your finances in the general admissions process. They do, however, consider your need for college-sponsored financial aid, especially if you are on the margin for acceptance. Here are some of the benefits to winning merit-based scholarships:

1. If you go after scholarships that are not college based, your chances of getting admitted are greater.

2. If you win scholarships, you're EFC (Estimated Family Contribution) increases and your need for need-based aid decreases.

3. By holding outside merit scholarships, the school will first reduce the need for subsidized loan packages before reducing any need-based grants. Therefore, the only thing you are losing out on is the assumption of more debt. Not a bad thing.

4. Your need-based grants are increased due to "preferential packaging" policies.

5. Since financial aid officers can determine aid on a case-by-case basis, the fact that you took the initiative to win outside merit scholarships gives you the opportunity to persuade them to improve your aid package.

6. Many schools have created "matching scholarships", in which they will provide an additional scholarship to each student who brings in an outside scholarship.

7. Scholarship money is usually not taxed. You should always ask your tax advisor about this.

CHAPTER 18

Parent Support During the Scholarship Search

1. Volunteer work in high schools can provide parents with access to CD ROMS, scholarship files, and the opportunity to talk to the high school counselor. Information about scholarships start arriving into the counselors office in the early fall and continue for quite a few months. Some deadlines are within weeks of the fall notification and some will not be due until after January of that year. Making a list of possible scholarships and their deadlines helps the student to arrange scholarship time around school and other activities. This way, the parent can know and help with the organization of these lists. Remember though, the student is the one who should be filling out the forms and writing the essays. You as a parent can critique and be your student's moral support. Even if you work, counselors are more than willing to share the scholarship information with you. Calling the high school office is helpful. Not only do you benefit, but so does the school in terms of strong public relations.

2. Making phone calls or handling letter writing or requesting forms can be done by the parents. (In writing a request letter for a scholarship form, make sure you address the letter to a specific person or the coordinator. Also, include all your information, name, address, all phone numbers, fax number and e-mail address to make it easy for the receiver to respond. Also, you can include a self addressed, stamped envelope to ensure a quick turnaround.) Your involvement assures that the student will be more willing to participate and follow through when he/she can see that the family is all working together and he/she has your support. Also, students are in school from approximately 8 a.m. to 3 p.m. and aren't able to make calls or order forms.

3. Essay writing is an especially difficult task. Not only has the student been writing for college applications, but he/she is now faced with a new set of essay challenges. Help with any research that needs to be done, including brainstorming about subjects to write about.

4. Look back in graduation- printed materials to find scholarships won by previous students.

5. Talk to seniors about the scholarships they are pursuing.

6. Look for scholarships that are not obvious. If you dig hard enough, they can be found. If many people don't know about them, there will be fewer entries and your odds for winning are significantly increased.

7. Pay close attention to your organizations and church affiliations. Even tap their national organization.

8. Most of all, realize that many of the scholarships that are applied for will not be won. Recognize that a student may apply for twenty scholarships. If he/she wins one, this is just a five per cent success rate. Be supportive and help the student stay enthusiastic about continuing to try. So many wonderful character traits can

be developed during this process. Not only will your student learn more about himself or herself, but will learn about family teamwork and the values of impacting their own destiny.

CHAPTER 19

Competing in the Application Process

Listed by priorities of the colleges and universities:

1. **GPA**—Your high school calculates your GPA. AP and honors courses are sometimes given weight up to a point extra for the letter grade. For example, an "A" usually counts as four points, but if weighted will count five points. Colleges may ask for weighted and unweighted GPA scores. They will decide if the weight will be kept or if a percentage will be used in calculating the admissions GPA. Because honors classes do not follow a standardized curriculum, the weight may be dropped. Also, GPA counted in admissions in most colleges is only taken from core classes and academic electives. *Class rank is considered by many colleges, but unfortunately is unfavorable for private school students. This is due to the smaller number of students in the class and the larger number of students who compete with GPAs that are separated by a fraction of a point.*

2. **Curriculum**—Curriculum should be challenging and will affect the weight of the GPA in the college selection process.

3. **Standardized Testing**—Prepare to take these tests, beginning with the PSAT and the PLAN. It is important to sign up for the SAT I, SAT II and ACT tests as soon as you know your available testing date. It is advisable to practice the sample tests a couple of months before the testing. Practice tests can be found in the practice booklet available in the counselor's office, and online at ***www.collegeboard.com***, ***www.act.org*** and ***www.fastweb.com***. You must not only practice the tests, but look for test taking hints from these sites. Practice helps you perform faster, which is a large factor for success on these tests. Testing can be practiced in the beginning of the junior year, but, the recommendation by the College Board and the American College Testing is to start testing in the spring of the junior year and continue through the early fall for best academic results. SAT II are subject tests that are required by certain colleges and universities. College handbooks have these listings as well as the web page of each school.

4. **Essay**—This part of the application conveys the student's ability to express himself or herself creatively and shows the reader who the student is. Humor can be used in light doses, but tread carefully. The reader is not a teenager.

5. **Personal Development**—This can range from creating a position of leadership to extending your education by studying abroad. It's a very important element in the application process, especially for select schools and scholarships. This will help separate one student over another when GPA and standardized scores are close

6. **Resumé** —This list does not have to be a laundry list of clubs and organizations. It can be just as impressive to participate in a few activities and hold positions of leadership throughout and during the years in high school. It is not the quantity, but the

quality. Many colleges will have student's list activities by order of interest to them. In these cases, it is not necessary to send a resumé. You can develop your own grid that will allow you room for details. Using Microsoft Word, you click on "Table" function on the main menu. Then click on "Insert Table" and set the rows and columns to make a chart. You can move the lines to make room for the Description column. *The key is the depth and breadth, not quantity. The activity list is the most crucial part of your application because it establishes your talents, passions, interest level, and impact on your community.*

7. **Letters of Recommendation**—These letters offer additional information about *the student* which helps the college representative reading the application to understand who this student is in terms of character as well as classroom participation and involvement. It is very important to choose the person who will write the recommendation in terms of two things:

   a. He/she must know *the student* well.

   b. He/she should be a good writer.

Honesty and Integrity are important in compiling your personal data. College Admissions Counselors are smart and experienced enough to cross reference the student's leadership and references report with the teacher/counselor recommendations.

Interviews

Interviews are not used very often, but visiting the school and making an appointment with a college counselor (one that represents your state and/ or will read your application) will show your interest in that college as well as place a face with a name for the admissions counselor. Interviewing for scholarships is usually done as an invitation and is done mostly in person and occasionally by phone.

Auditions

Auditions include the performing arts, oratorical scholarships, or a formal presentation of scientific findings through a student's research.

Portfolios

Portfolios should be prepared far in advance of the deadline and be guided by an art teacher. The format for putting a portfolio together is very precise. It is very important to work directly with the art teacher in presenting your work. It is equally important to complete your works ahead of the deadline to avoid having to spend time when you may not have it. Thus, you can think through what you choose to submit and you can make changes, if needed. When you coordinate your works early, you can enjoy the feeling of satisfaction without the high rush of panic!

Advanced Placement Courses

AP courses are offered in most high schools, some offering many more options than others. A college is looking for student's selection within the AP offerings at their high school. The number is important, but the variety is just as important, if not more. If a student chooses to take three or four AP's, all in separate areas of interest (Math, English, Science, Foreign Language, and History), the student will be more likely to work on a college level and therefore the college will weigh this in terms of how they predict the student's success at this particular college. Selecting APs across the different areas of study is better than choosing three science APs or two English APs.

In the event that a student cannot take an AP class due to scheduling or an unfavorable teacher choice, he/she can choose to take the AP exam. The student can buy the preparation booklet for a particular AP subject (found in local book stores) and schedule to take the test in their high school.

Non-AP Curriculum

Students are not always proficient in all areas, but do spread the selection around. For some students, APs are not the best choice for various reasons:

a. In academic performance, the student may be average.

b. The student hasn't the time for the extra work entailed in AP courses.

c. The student does not wish to live under this kind of pressure in high school.

d. The student does not desire colleges or universities that require APs as a competitive edge in applying.

Students who choose not to take APs can challenge themselves in many other ways. In choosing electives, try to choose academic electives such as Psychology, Physics, Chemistry, Pre-cal, Calculus, Honors English and History, 3 – 5 years of a foreign language, etc.

CHAPTER 20

Show Who You Are

Motivated student: Take practice tests found online.

Unmotivated student: Consider a Prep Course like Stanley Kaplan or Princeton Review provided at a local college. Or, hire a private tutor (adult or upperclassman that scored well on the test).

Think of admissions to a college the same as interviewing for a job.

- Resumé presented.

- Your prior experiences noted.

- Your first impressions weighed.

- Your verbal presentation weighed.

- Your enthusiasm noticed.

- Your knowledge of the area of the job or position, noted.

- Your interest in that position noted.

- Your presented attitude is weighed.

- Your education level is weighed (formal and informal).

- Your overall appearance is noted.

- Your opinion on ethical practice or how to approach problems.

This entire list is about who you are. How much you have accomplished, devoted your time to, prioritized your commitments, endured, juggled, etc. The same holds true for applying to colleges, especially competitive ones. In an admissions office, your character matters no matter how strong your application may be. Within your numbers (GPA and standardized scores), and core curriculum, you will look similar to other applicants. It may open the door to admissions for you, but, it is important to show who you are through:

- Your intellectual curiosity and passion.

- Your willingness to "go outside the box" in your interests and/or abilities.

- The enthusiasm *you* show in your essays and interviews.

- Showing *one's* passionate interests to inspire outside learning.

- *Your intellectual curiosity and passion* can be shown based on books you've read. Anything you're interested in- things might range from interest in politics to football. A person who is interested in something will usually show it by actively reading about it, listening to programs, writing about it after doing some research, participating in it, and being generally inspired to learn all they can. If you are interested in:

  a. **Math**—You can tutor, assist a teacher with a project, read about math related fields and choose one that interests you, like engineering, etc.

  b. **History**—You might show an interest in how people over time have contributed to culture and society. Through this, you can zero in on an individual time in history or focus on leaders and their impact on society. You can then begin to study, read, and learn about society today. The most important thing that you do is to get involved in the community.

- **_Going outside the box_** is so important for personal development as well as for being admitted to a college or earning a scholarship. Some ways in which a student can show this are the following:

    a. **Academically**—If you are interested in taking a fourth year language and it is not offered at your school, you may consider dual enrollment in a local college. This shows initiative which can result in a recommendation from the college professor, not to mention college credit. It shows that you can succeed in a college setting as well.

    b. **Computers**—If a student is proficient and interested in computer technology, he/she should expand on that to show going beyond knowledge and usage. The student could take an adult oriented several hour course to learn to trouble shoot, upgrade and fix computers and apprentice with a computer technician. At the same time, he/she could become certified.

    c. **Hobbies**—Colleges will remember students with unusual and strange hobbies. Directors of admissions like to include in their final report of the incoming freshman class that they have the nation's top debater, a fire thrower, a champion mogul jumper, a published author, a nationally recognized poet, or a CEO of a start-up e-mail business. Other non -academic hobbies could and should include activities such as: mountain climbing, skeet shooting, stargazing, sport fishing, collecting stamps and/or coins, baking, cooking, etc.

As mentioned in Chapter 6, students who used their math, sports, and music abilities to implement "going outside the box", you too can use these or any talents or interests you have. These experiences or ones of your choice can be used on your resumé as well as in your essays. This will show your traits (initiative, creativity, caring, commitment, effort, persistence, etc.)

To a college, a student's initiative and achievement shows a serious time commitment and a love of learning. In general, colleges want high-impact recruits who will represent an investment, who will make a difference and will be remembered years later. The so-called well-rounded student focus has changed to the well-rounded freshman class.

You should be authentic in your enthusiasm. The way in which your attitude is expressed on paper or in person may help to make you stand out to the admissions counselors. Project your energy and enthusiasm for your passions.

In an essay or in an interview, think beforehand about how you truly feel about a subject or interest. Use your own ideas this way and write or say something that is original and from the heart. It is important to think beyond the simple.

CHAPTER 21

Admissions "To Do" List

To remain organized during this application process, keep a folder with inside pockets for each college.

Individual College Applications

Print out all sheets that include:

- The application itself (**you** submit)

- School Report Form (**student** gives to the school counselor)

- Mid-year Report Form (**student** gives to the school counselor)

- Teacher Recommendation Forms, if included

- Final Year Report Form (student gives to school counselor)

The Common Application
(found on college websites or at
www.commonapp.com.)

Print out all sheets that include:

- The application itself (you submit).

- School Report Form (given to the school counselor).

- Mid-Year Report Form (given to the school counselor).

- Two Teacher Recommendation Forms.

- Final Year Report Form (given to the school counselor).

- Print out the "supplement" to each college found on their website.

Generally:

- Print out or record dates and deadlines (include Early Decision, Early Action, and Regular Decision dates.)

- Print out or record SAT II requirements.

- Print out any scholarship forms (note automatic ones and deadlines.)

- Print out honors college form and note deadlines.

- Print out specific department scholarship forms and note deadlines.

Financial Aid

To be sent by parents:

- The **FAFSA** ("Free" Application for Student Aid) website (to be sent, beginning in January) Note "Free." Watch out for scams. The only website to use is: ***www.fafsa.ed.gov***.

- The **CSS Profile** (if requested by the College) **Send by deadline**.

- Any specific financial aid form provided by and requested by the college

Note dates and deadlines of these forms. Keep copies of all materials sent.

Testing

1. Schedule to take the **SAT I** and/or **ACT** (note deadlines and schedule early online to ensure desired testing location).

2. Schedule **SAT II's** (note deadlines and dates given, as well as requirements made by your colleges of choice). It is best to take these tests after taking the course.

3. When registering, send scores to as many schools as the form will allow (for free) and pay for additional ones:

   a. ACT—Any additional schools are $9.00 per score per school. You must request each testing date that you want to be sent.

   b. SAT I & SAT II—Any additional schools listed will cost $9.50 per score per school.

Make sure all scores are sent directly from ACT and/or SAT to the colleges of your choice. Prices are subject to change.

Sports

Register with the NCAA Clearing House before you begin your college sport. Forms found online or in the high school counseling office.

Armed Forces

Recommendation requirements begin in the spring of your junior year.

1. Print out and save any forms you send.

2. Check on the college website for confirmation of materials.

CHAPTER 22

The Interview Process

The college interview is a time for information gathering and for the admission officer to "sell the college experience" rather than evaluating the student. As a student, you should be relaxed and happy, but arrive with information about the college. Also, think beforehand about your personal school experience and have knowledge about your high school such as how many APs are offered, size of the classroom, activities offered, etc. You know yourself best, so share who you are with the interviewer without embellishing yourself. Also, think about your future plans in connection with the college opportunities for career, educational exposure, internships, and later job opportunities. You need to know how this college will play a part in your plans.

The obvious question is: "Why are you interested in this college?" You could mention that after looking at the catalogue you were interested in the idea of double majoring in Spanish and German." Or perhaps, after a college visit you were impressed with the school's interior design curriculum. Make sure that part of your answer is *ACADEMIC* in nature.

Since the interviewer will have a copy of your transcript, you need to think about your academic experience. For instance, the question could be, "Why did you receive a 'C' in chemistry when you are planning to major in Pre-Med?" Be ready with an academic explanation. Perhaps, "I was encouraged by my counselor to take the more difficult Advanced Chemistry instead of the lower level—I thought I was prepared, and I worked hard in the class, but, I just didn't have enough foundation. The important thing is that I learned a lot, earned a 700 on the chemistry SAT II, and discovered that I can take a risk, do poorly, and live through it."

The interviewer will usually ask what you want to know about the college. In most cases, the interviewer will ask "What do you want to know about our college?" This is your BIG CHANCE to make a really good impression. Have a few notes with you to reassure yourself. Ask FIRST AND FOREMOST about the academic program you are interested in. Then ask about the secondary academic programs (study abroad, double major, internships, and externships. Finally, ask about the recreational interests you have (remember, in the "mind" of the college, you are attending for ACADEMIC reasons). If you need tutorial support or disabilities services, this is a good time to find out if the college can meet your needs.

Remember, a terrible or wonderful interview will not depend solely on a wonderful or terrible academic record. Ultimately, you will be judged by the "whole picture" of your application. So, relax and enjoy using this time to learn more about the place where you might spend the next four years.

Hints:

- Read the view book and other materials before the interview.

- Review your transcript.

- Be prepared to answer questions about your academic history and special talents or interests.

- Dress neatly, be on time, be honest, look at the interviewer and speak distinctly. Thank the interviewer before leaving.

You can perform a "mock interview" with a counselor or your parents to prepare for this process. As an *independent counselor*, I hold mock interviews with my students.

Questions Students are Often Asked at a College Interview

- "How did you first hear about our college?"

- "What are your career goals, including long- range and short-range plans?"

- "What are you interested in majoring in?"

- "What kinds of things do you do outside of school?"

- "What have you accomplished, or what activities have you participated in that have had a particular effect on you and your life?"

- "What are your academic strengths and weaknesses?"

- "How familiar are you with this college and its programs?"

- "Which one of your activities has given you the most satisfaction?"

- "If you had high school to do over again, would you do anything differently?"

- "What particular life goals are you seeking to achieve or pursue?"

- "What are your priorities in selecting a college?"

- "How would you describe your high school and how would you change it?"

- "Where do you see yourself in four years?"

- "Discuss your most stimulating intellectual experience."

- "Tell me about something you have really wanted which you had to go after on your own."

- "What is the most significant contribution you have made to your school?"

- "What books or articles have made a lasting impression on your way of thinking?"

- "Have you read deeply into any author or field?"

- "Have you ever thought of not going to college?" If so, what would you do?"

- "Among people you have known, whom do you admire the most?"

Off the Wall Questions

- "If you were a color, which color would you be and why?"

- "If you had three wishes, what would they be?"

- "If you could meet an historical figure, who would it be and why?"

- "What three items do you always carry in your pockets/purse/book bag/glove compartment?"

- "If you had to write a letter to the President of the United States, what would you say and why?"

- "If you could rewrite the ending of the last novel you read or the last movie you watched, how would you change it and why?"

Questions About Your Transcript/Resumé

- "I see you made lower grades in English. What do you attribute this to?"

- "Your activities are heavily concentrated in soccer. Do you plan to pursue this?"

Eleven Tips for the Admissions and Scholarship Interview

1. Learn as much as you can about the college before you visit. Be prepared to both answer and ask questions.

2. Give some advance thought to things you want to look for and ask about. Having a list of questions with you is acceptable.

3. Go alone, rather than with a friend or a group. Your parent(s) can go along for the drive, but they should not participate in the admissions or scholarship interview. Parents are sometimes invited to speak with the admissions officer following the interview.

4. Arrive on time or a few minutes early. ***DO NOT BE LATE!***

5. Be yourself at all times—be honest, sincere, interested.

6. Know your background and experience. Be prepared to present it in an orderly manner.

7. Smile. Speak distinctly. Look at the interviewer when you are speaking.

8. State and defend opinions ***ONLY*** if asked. Do not be argumentative. If you do not know something, admit it. Do not try to bluff.

9. Dress neatly, conservatively, and attractively.

10. Relax. Interviews are meant to be informative to both parties. Try to get as much out of the interview as you put into it.

11. Thank your interviewer for his/her time and consideration. Write a thank you note of appreciation. This shows thoughtfulness, courtesy, and maturity. It reinforces the admissions/scholarship officer's memory of you as an individual.

Things Not to do During an Interview

- Don't look at your watch (an interview can be as short as fifteen minutes).

- Don't leave your cell phone on or put it on vibrate.

- Don't be restless.

- Don't pick or bite your nails.

- Don't slouch in the chair.

- Don't yawn.

- Don't constantly straighten your clothing.

CHAPTER 23

The College Visit

Suggestions for College Visits

1. Plan time to visit when high school is not in session and college is.

2. In your inquiry, request a definite date and time.

3. Be on time! If you must cancel, notify the admissions office as soon as you can.

4. Make an appointment with the admissions office for a tour. Connect with a specific counselor when calling, specifically one that will read your area's applications and make an appointment to speak with him/her upon your arrival. After speaking with him or her, you may be transferred to another counselor for scheduling the actual tour. Scheduling a college campus tour can be done either by calling the college visitors center or registering for a tour online.

5. You can make arrangements through the admissions office to stay overnight in a dorm and attend a class (preferably

a freshman class). This is very appropriate in the fall of your senior year.

6. Arrange other appointments specific to your needs or interests (financial aid office, special needs, a specific major or department, the athletic department, etc.)

7. You should write a thank you to everyone who took the time to meet with you. Remember, every time they see your name, it adds to your profile. "The squeaking wheel gets the grease."

College Visit Questions for Students

Academics

1. Are students taught by full- time faculty members, graduate assistants, or a combination of the two?

2. What is the average class size? Largest? Smallest?

3. How many students in last year's freshman class returned for their sophomore year?

4. What was the grade point average for the freshman class last year?

5. What is the college's procedure for student orientation, class placement, and scheduling?

6. Do you require SAT II tests for admission or class placement and if so, which ones?

7. How is a faculty advisor assigned to students?

8. What services does the school offer for the student who is undecided about a major?

9. How many students complete a degree?

10. Do students graduate in four or five years?

11. What are the most popular majors?

12. What are your support systems for students with a learning disability?

13. What types of additional services are provided by the school at no additional cost to the student (tutoring, career and personal counseling, developmental reading, student skills workshops, or job placement)?

14. Is there an honors program? What are the qualifications for entry? When do you apply?

15. What are the strongest departments at the college?

16. What is the percentage of students who are accepted into postgraduate studies?

Admission Policies

1. What high school courses are recommended and/or required?

2. Do you prefer/require the ACT or the SAT? What range of scores is accepted?

3. Does the college require a certain GPA?

4. How much weight will my activities and involvement in school be given?

5. Is there an essay on the application and how much importance is it given?

6. Do you have early decision and how does it work?

7. What are your main criteria for admissions?

8. Are personal interviews or letters of recommendation required?

9. Are there specific requirements for certain majors?

10. What percent of applicants are accepted?

11. Can admission denials be appealed?

12. What are the application/scholarship deadlines?

13. Is a student's application used automatically for scholarships or does the student need to apply separately?

14. When will the college notify me that I qualify for a scholarship interview?

About the College

1. What is the surrounding community like?

2. Is the college public, private, or church affiliated?

3. What is the current school enrollment?

4. What special or unique programs are offered, such as study abroad?

5. Does the college have general courses that are required for all freshmen? What are they?

6. How large is the library and what is the computer availability?

7. What support services are available to students? General counseling? Post –graduate planning? Free health care? Tutoring, if needed?

8. Is there assistance in finding off-campus employment during the school year and during the summer or junior year study abroad?

Student Population

1. Where are the majority of students from (in-state, out-of-state)? Male/female ratio?

2. What percentage of students lives on campus?

3. What types of student activities are available?

4. How big are sororities and fraternities on campus?

5. Do freshmen have to live on campus?

6. Can freshmen have cars (if so, what is the procedure for a parking permit)?

7. What is the average size of the freshman class?

8. Is there summer orientation?

9. Are intramural sports available? If so, which ones?

10. What kind of student is generally the most successful/happy at this college?

Social Life

1. Are dorms co-ed or single sex?

2. How soon can you register for a dorm?

3. What kind of meal plan is there on campus?

4. Is this a "suitcase college" (students leave on weekends)?

5. What are the procedures for selecting a roommate?

6. What are some of the rules and regulations that govern campus and dormitory life?

7. What kinds of cultural, sports or literary activities are offered on campus?

8. Are there special dorms for honors students, or areas of interests?

College Costs

1. What are the costs for tuition? Room and board? How much did costs increase from last year to this year?

2. What is the difference in cost for in-state and out-of-state students?

3. Are accepted students required to place deposits for tuition and housing? Are these refundable?

4. Is May 1 the accepted date to accept student decision for admissions and scholarships complying with the Students Rights and Responsibilities?

Financial Aid

1. What percent of students receive financial aid based on financial need?

2. What percent of students receive scholarships based on academic ability?

3. What would be a typical financial aid package for a freshman?

4. What percent of students that apply for financial aid receive it?

5. What are the financial aid procedures and deadlines (FAFSA, CSS PROFILE)?

6. Do you have a personal financial aid form to be submitted?

Have prior knowledge of the answers to some of these questions. Go online and read about the college facts and also, read college handbooks.

CHAPTER 24

College Websites

1. The College Board ....www.collegeboard.com
- SAT preparation
- Registration for SAT (Dates and costs)
- College and Scholarship search
- CSS Profile online

2. ACT ....www.act.org
- Registration for ACT
- Dates and cost

3. Fast Web .... www.fastweb.com

4. FAFSA .... www.fafsa.ed.gov
- Financial Aid Form

5. Finaid ....www.finaid.com
- Calculates the EFC (Estimated Family Contribution)

6. CSS Profile .... www.profileonline.com

7. Common Application .... www.commonapp.org

8. Colleges .... www.(name of college).edu

9. NCAA .... www.ncaa.org

CHAPTER 25

The Answer

1. **Deferred**—When colleges hold onto your admissions for a period of time. The student should call the college admissions office to get a sense of any weakness in the application process and what advice they have for him/her. The student can emphasize his/her interest in that school. The student can hope that his/her new grades will help. You can have an extra recommendation sent.

2. **Accepted**—When colleges accept you as a future student in their freshman class, you have until May 1 of your senior year to respond. For the colleges that you decide not to attend, it is appropriate for you to contact them, either by e-mail or letter and notify them of your plans to attend another college.

3. **Wait-Listed**—If you have been wait-listed, do not depend on being selected. You should notify one of your acceptances by May 1 and not depend on the wait-listed school. If you are notified by the weight-listed school of your acceptance after May 1, you can accept their offer and then contact the school that you accepted originally.

4. **Denied**—If you have been denied by a school, you can call them about an appeal. The school may not consider your request for the appeal, but it is worth trying. If the appeal is possible, the school will ask you to send additional information that was not included in you original application.

CHAPTER 26

Why Use a Higher Education Consultant?

The high school years are a time when students and families are looking beyond to their plans for higher education. As students approach their junior year, they begin a process that can be overwhelming. High schools, unfortunately, are often unable to provide the individualized attention needed for each student. It's important to search for colleges that fit your student, academically as well as socially. An independent counselor has the time to provide individualized services to the student and family with all details of the college admission process. The independent counselor will help to match a student to the right college. Considerations include the student's academics, scoring, special talents, interest, character and personality, as well as the student's maturity, needs and wants, academically and socially. The independent counselor works for **you**, the student and family. He/she also has great knowledge about colleges and the admission process. In addition, he/she is able to contact colleges on behalf of the student.

Time

Time is a factor that should be considered when hiring an independent counselor. It is often hard for parents to find the time necessary to gather all the details and facts needed to understand the competition among colleges.

Mediator

Acting as a mediator between student and family, the independent counselor is able to effectively help the student prepare for admissions and inform the family of this progress. By working as a family unit, it makes the entire process easier for all involved.

Application

The application should present the student in his/her most attractive manner. From filling it out correctly (no spelling errors), to writing a dynamic essay that reveals the student, it is a very important piece. It is the student's chance to show who they are and how they fit that particular college.

Personal Development

As an independent counselor, I've found this category to be critically important to the student and to the college application process. Helping the student expand upon their talents and interests as well as learn or refine life skills, teaches students to use their abilities to the maximum and to use strategy in achieving goals (in this case, admission to a college of choice).

College Connections

The independent counselor is in the business of knowing the colleges and the admission counselors well. These vital connections allow the independent counselor the opportunity to contact those associated with the colleges on behalf of the student.

My Experience

In the many years that I was a counselor working in a private high school, I felt that parents had invested time and money to help their high school students reach the goal of being accepted in the college of their choice. I had children in public and private schools. In both situations I was involved with the total college application process. The most difficult problem was the *amount of time required*. With my first two children, admissions were not as competitive as they became for my last two. The admissions process had not only become more rigid, but the rules of the game had changed and become more competitive in nature. There were issues such as selecting the number of AP Courses needed to apply to competitive schools, learning to write an essay, knowing which schools and how many to apply, to learning good interviewing skills, and keeping the time line for the all dates required. Questions that parents and students began to ask: "Should a student apply early decision (ED), early action (EA) or regular decision? Which one will give the student a better chance for admission?" "Will I qualify for federal aid if I fill out the FAFSA, and when do I do this?" In addition, the ACT, SAT I and SATII, created a great deal of stress in deciding how best to prepare.

I learned an enormous amount about the college process and family dynamics during that time. Even though I was a counselor during my last two children's search for a college, I was unable to emotionally separate myself from the situation. At that time, I wished that I had another professional to help.

It was soon after my last child left for college that I became an independent counselor. My experience with my children plus my interest in families prompted my decision to start my own business; College Counseling Services, L.L.C (CCS).

I maintained membership with NACAC (National Association of College Admission Counselors) and SACAC (Southern Association of Admission Counselors). After starting CCS, I joined IECA (Independent Education Counseling Association) and HECA (Higher Education Counseling Association). I applied for and earned my CEP (Certified Educational Planner), but after five years, I decided not to renew my certification. I felt the demands for excessive travel were not as valuable as spending that time with my students.

When I started CCS, I began to speak to groups of parents and students about what the college application process would entail. I began traveling to visit many colleges and universities around the country (which I continually do presently) and made valuable contacts with admissions departments. As I continued my professional relationships with college counselors and other department heads, I learned how valuable these contacts were for students and their families.

As an independent counselor, I found that I have more time to help students with self- improvement and enrichment of their talents, while providing support for their parents too. As a high school counselor, I "wore too many hats" which prevented me from having the time to devote to the college-bound student.

For the last six years, I have been an independent counselor. In that time, I have helped public, private school, and home-schooled students. The needs of both the students and parents do not vary between those in private school, public school or those home-schooled. What does vary is the degree of help and guidance needed. Not only have my students benefited from help with the applications, but they have learned to think about themselves, positively and critically and learned how to use their strengths and improve their weaknesses before going to college.

CHAPTER 27

Glossary for College Applicants

ACT—The American College Testing program is a standardized college entrance test offered to high school juniors and seniors on various dates listed online at ***www.act.org*** or in a high school counselor's office. This test consists of four parts: English, math, reading, and science reasoning. You must request that ACT send all of your scores to each school. In each report, ACT will only send that most recent score and no other scores from other test dates. You are basically tested on how you evaluate and process information.

SAT I—The abbreviation for the standardized college entrance test offered by the College Board. The Scholastic Aptitude Test is offered on a number of dates and consists of two parts: critical reading and math. In addition there is a writing portion. Tests are scored on a scale of 200 – 800 points per section. Registration forms are in high school guidance offices as well as online ***www.collegeboard.com***. You are basically tested on how you evaluate and process information.

SAT II—includes a series of sixteen subject-area exams sponsored by the Educational Testing Service (ETS). Students may take one, two, or three exams on test date (one hour test each). The scores provide a national standard to measure a student's performance in classroom achievement. Test subjects include areas such as English Composition, English Literature, American History, European History, Math, Latin, Spanish, Biology, Chemistry, and Physics. Tests are scored on a scale of 200 – 800 points. Forms can be found in high school guidance offices and online at *www.collegeboard.com*. Unlike the SAT I, you are tested on your knowledge of each subject. Some colleges require a certain number to be taken and/or specify certain ones. Check on the college website for that information. If you have just finished a course in a particular subject, it is advisable to take that particular subject test at that time.

Advanced Placement (AP)—A series of exams offered in classroom subject areas taken in May each year. Many high schools offer AP courses in many subject areas. Students may earn from one to five college credits depending on the score earned on the test (scores on a scale from 1 – 5). The colleges determine what score will earn college credit.

Candidate's Reply Date—May 1 has been designated as the date by which all students must make a commitment to the college he or she will attend in the fall. Many schools will notify a student of admission before April 15 (the last date the colleges must inform students about their applications), but no student seeking admission under Regular Decision need notify a college of attendance before May 1.

CEEB—The College Entrance Examination Board is a nonprofit organization governed by college and secondary school members. CEEB is the overseeing agency for many tests and services connected with the college admission process.

CLEP—The College Level Examination Program sponsored by the College Board through which students can receive credit for class work experiences and on-the-job training. Not all colleges recognize CLEP credit.

College—(as different from a university) An educational institution that offers instruction beyond the high-school level in a two or four year program only, or an academic division of a university, such as the College of Arts and Sciences.

University—A university is an institution of higher education and research, which grants academic degrees in a variety of subjects. A university provides both undergraduate education and postgraduate education.

College Board—A nonprofit organization whose membership includes colleges and universities and a large number of secondary schools. It offers a wide variety of services to members, including standardized admission and financial aid procedures, guidelines for admission policy, and a forum to discuss topics of concern to the higher education community.

College Representative—Many colleges send admission officers to high schools to promote their schools and introduce their programs to prospective students.

College Scholarship Service (CSS)—The division of the College Board responsible for the PROFILE and the needs analysis that determines the family's contribution toward payment of a student's education.

Common Application—The Common Application is a form that can be used to apply to over 100 private colleges; college applicants need to fill out only one form. Duplicates of the form serve as applications to participating colleges. Supplements can be found on the college websites.

Co-Op Program—In a cooperative program between a college and a corporation, studio, or lab, the student attends classes and then works off-campus, for pay, at the business site in the student's career field to gain experience.

Deferred Admission—Is a process by which high school students apply for and are accepted for admission to colleges during their senior year. They may choose to enter as freshman after a one-year absence from school. A deferred admission is a commitment on the part of the college to take the student: a deferred acceptance is a commitment on the part of the student to attend after one year. Check with the college for specifics on deferring your enrollment.

Early Action—This is a decision plan allowing students to apply to school(s) early, and, in return, the college(s) responds with an admission decision early in the cycle. It differs from Early Decision because Early Action is nonbinding. Check with the schools to which you are applying to see which decision plans they offer.

Early Admission—Many colleges have a program under which a student may apply for admission during the junior year. Early Admission at most colleges is reserved for truly exceptional individuals whose academic preparation, achievement level, and maturity level are sufficient.

Early Decision (ED)—This is an early application process that involves a binding agreement on the part of the student. If a student is admitted under ED, he or she agrees to enroll at a particular college and to withdraw all other applications in process at other schools. This option is a good plan for students who have a clear first choice and are willing to stand on academic and extracurricular records through their junior year. ED deadlines vary from school to school. Students not admitted under Early Decision are usually, but not always, reconsidered with Regular Decision applicants.

Regular Decision—This is the most common admission program. Applications for admission are due sometime between January 1 and January 15 at most selective colleges; applicants are notified of their admission status between April 1 and April 15.

Rolling Admission—This means that as soon as an application arrives at a college, the admission office starts evaluating them and making decisions, often within three or four weeks. Usually, if you are accepted under this plan, you will not have to commit yourself until May 1. Most, but not all state universities operate with Rolling Admissions; the earlier you apply, the better the chance for acceptance at most colleges using this plan. Occasionally, a state university may decide to set a standard (a certain GPA and ACT/SAT I) for summer and early fall applications. Check to make sure before applying early.

Need Blind Admission—Need- blind schools make admission decisions completely without regard to each student's ability to pay for the costs of the institution.

FAFSA—The Free Application for Federal Student Aid form is available from the high school guidance office as well as online at ***www.fafsa.ed.gov***. Be sure to use only this web site. If a similar website asks for money to process this form, it is a scam.

Liberal Arts—A broad undergraduate program of education stressing the core courses: pre-professional training is also available.

Arts And Sciences—A college's Liberal Arts School (usually the largest school). Liberal Arts are not engineering, business, pharmacy, or nursing. They consist of the humanities; physical, life, and natural sciences: math: and social science disciplines.

Melt—This is the effect of having students forfeit their enrollment deposits over the summer months before actually arriving at college. This happens for a number of reasons: students decide not to go to college at all or students are removed from the wait list at a first-choice school.

Merit Scholarships—Money given to students to cover college expenses without regard for financial need; athletic scholarships, academic scholarships, music scholarships, dance scholarships, etc.

Super Scoring—Colleges will take the highest sub score of the Critical Reading and Math sections of the SAT I and recalculate a composite score that will be used in admissions. This is why it is wise to take the SAT I several times and submit each testing results to your colleges of choice.

Notes

Notes

Notes

Notes

Notes

Notes